HEY GUYS!

It's

SOME THINGS I WANT TO SHARE
BEFORE I NO LONGER CAN

ANDY BLASQUEZ

ISBN: 979-8-9876663-0-2 (Paperback)
ISBN: 979-8-9876663-1-9 (Hardcover)
ISBN: 979-8-9876663-2-6 (eBook)

Cover Concept: Andy Blasquez, Michael Blasquez, & Jeffrey Blasquez.
Book Interior Layout & ebook Conversion by manuscript2ebook.com

The information presented herein represents the author's view at the date and time of publication. This book is presented for informational purposes only. Due to the rate at which the hard and soft sciences change, the author reserves the right to alter, edit, and update his thoughts and opinions based on new knowledge. While every attempt has been made to recall accurately, express, and reflect on his authentic experiences in this book, neither the author nor any entity affiliated with this book will assume any responsibility for errors, inaccuracies, or omissions.

Dedication

This book is very sincerely dedicated to anyone and everyone who finds support, guidance, peace, and/or love in the words that follow.

The creation of this book was inspired by my loving family. I appreciate your support, your patience, your understanding, and most importantly, your faith in me and your love for me.

To my beautiful, kind, and resilient sons, Michael and Jeffrey: this book, this culmination, this life…I do it all for you.

Contents

PART 1
Learn & Grow—A Memoir

PART 2
Share—The "It's Dad" Blogs

A Note to the Reader

The material in this book—my background, clinical information, physical and emotional traumas, how this whole project got started, my coping mechanisms, solutions, perspectives, the tools and skills that helped me find peace, and so much more—is all interwoven in a sort of multidimensional matrix of experiences and knowledge and life. It wasn't until the editing stage of this book that it became clear just how challenging it would be to organize these thoughts and ideas in a logical, chronological, or easy-to-follow manner. That task was not only far beyond my skills as a writer but beyond my mentors' considerable skills as well. So, I apologize in advance for the wanderings and rabbit holes that may appear to be completely disjointed, disconnected, or unrelated. I promise you that they aren't. Their relationships to each other are as connected as our moods are connected to our appetites.

Artists occasionally use the term "gestalt" to describe the idea that each element matters; each element is integral, but the whole is greater than the sum of its parts. I can assure you that each story from the first half of this book plays an integral role in the discoveries and applications shared in the second half…and beyond.

But before you dive deeper into the ideas within this book—especially the latter parts, the "teachings," if you will—I'll challenge you to slow down your reading, engage more deeply with the ideas, and draw parallels with experiences you've had and circumstances you're living within. These ideas aren't complete because they're only described from my personal perspective from one given point and time in my life. Overlaying your life's experiences onto mine (and those I've humbly learned from) might help facilitate and encourage unexpected growth and peace within your own life—and in turn, in the lives and relationships of those you care about most.

We're all different, with different attention spans, different approaches to learning, different ways of ruminating, pondering, resisting change, and digesting new points of view. For me personally, as topics and ideas get more and more complex, I find myself getting mentally or emotionally exhausted the more engaged I become. Sometimes, regardless of how eager I am to learn and grow, I'll feel as though I've been drinking through a firehose and I'm full. This requires me to read, listen, or watch things again and again—really understanding them for the first time, each time. There is no wrong way. I am humbled and grateful to think that something I've experienced, persevered through, and failed at countless times only to come out smiling in the end might help illuminate a path toward peace and joy for others.

Thank you.

Preface

*"Hope is the seed. Opportunity is the soil.
What we do with our opportunities determines how our flowers bloom."*

These lessons, paradigms, and stories come from my life. They come from years of pain, love, fear, exhilaration, abuse, and ultimately... finding peace. That's right: finding peace. I didn't "make it." I searched and learned and grew...and I discovered it.

I don't see peace as a destination or an arrival. I don't see it as the cliched "journey!" To me, it's not a journey or a destination. The best way I can describe my discovery of peace is the constant accrual of the skills, tools, and perspectives necessary to find the very best within any circumstance, with no occasion being more precious than another. Nothing is more precious than now.

These skills, tools, and perspectives afford me the calming certainty of knowing that regardless of conditions and circumstances, we can be happy. Once we've learned to practice and lean on the truths of these skills and to see things as *they* are rather than as *we* are...we realize that happiness is a choice. Yes, we will need (and life promises to give us) periodic reminders that happiness is right on the other side of changing our minds. Trust me; those humbling reminders will come. But it's true. Happiness is a choice.

It's the job of the universe to make waves. It's our job to learn how to surf 'em.

What to take away from this book: Learn. Grow. Share.

My mission and purpose for writing this book arose very slowly, sort of organically. Needing guidance to find patience and understanding, strength, confidence, and ultimately peace, I repeatedly turned to the most revered and inspirational spiritual leaders, mentors, sages, philosophers, and personal development coaches in history. From contemporaries such as Stephen Covey, Tony Robbins, and Eckhart Tolle to the Buddha and Siddhartha Gautama. From the Reverend Martin Luther King Jr. to the teachings of the Christian Bible, the Quran, and the Bhagavad Gita. From the ideas passed down from our most prolific Stoics to the time-tested fables of the Tao Te Ching.

I continue to read, engage, listen, watch, humble myself yet again... and learn.

This book dives into ideas and practices such as:

- How to be an excellent friend.
- The practice of creating space between stimulus and response.
- Recognizing that all stress stems from either the unwillingness or the inability to accept what is.
- Believing the fact that true joy will only ever be found inside.
- Being aware of our propensity to acquiesce to the values and opinions of others.
- How to find your voice (or perhaps allow your voice to find you)
- And so much more.

These perspectives…these habits…these actions and inactions… they complement each other. They're in alignment with each other. They align with the ideas found in every spiritual book I've ever read. They're timeless truths. They're dependable and durable. They are relevant in to-day's modern world precisely as they applied to life 200 or 500 or 3,000 years ago.

The rest of this book is sprinkled with new ideas, stories, experiences, perspectives, practices, fables, parables, and paradigm-shifting allegories, all of which continue to help my boys and me live our happiest, most peaceful and most fulfilled lives.

As Harvesting Insights continues to gain traction and attention, I'm reminded to stay humble and grateful and to remember my mission: *Learn. Grow. Share.*

The thoughts and words shared with you in this book are never final. The simple practice of weaving your own experiences within and between what is expressed in these pages proves just that. It's better… because of what you bring to it. So much better that I encourage you to reach out and share your thoughts and emotions with others and with me. We're better together. These words aren't written in stone but are steppingstones toward my next learning, growing, and sharing moments. All this on my way to leading a happier, more enlightened life. And, as ever, to shine a light for my boys, so they don't fall where I fell. So they and others might spend more of their lives in a place of peace and joy than I did.

Learn. Grow. Share.

That's why I'm here.

Part 1: Learn & Grow

A Memoir

1

Not Just Another School Day

Like clockwork, every weekday at 2:10 pm, it was time to put a thumbtack in my day and head to the elementary school. I'd park my truck at the bottom of a hill just below the school and walk up the hill to grab my boys. We'd run any necessary errands, then get ready for Little League practice, basketball, or whatever other typical All-American activities we had planned for the afternoon. It was spring—baseball season. I had one kid in the Minors, one in the Majors, and as ever...I was "Coach Dad." But today was different.

At the gate at the front of the school, a sea of excited but exhausted parents usually congregated, exchanging smiles and pleasantries before picking up their kids. On many days, those smiles and pleasantries were the only social interactions I'd have with adults other than the occasional, *"Thanks, Coach! See you Saturday."* I sincerely appreciated and looked forward to the friendly banter, but today was quieter than usual.

I had intentionally arrived about fifteen minutes early, hoping to pull Michael and Jeffrey out of class early, get 'em checked out at the office, out the door, and in the truck before the after-school rush.

As early as it was, there were only a handful of parents there. As soon as I walked through the gate, I heard a voice. It was a very deliberate, clear, stern voice speaking directly to me. Although I couldn't ignore it, I did my best to pretend I didn't hear whoever it was. I just wanted to go home. I wanted to be home. I tried in vain to ignore whoever was speaking to me, letting his words blend into the increasing number of *"Oohs"* and *"Oh-my-Gods"* coming from the handful of parents that were there.

As I gingerly limped toward the school office with blood oozing through the freshly applied gauze pads that sloppily covered my arms and legs, I kept saying to myself, almost tearfully pleading, *Please, please, please, help me get out of here early.*

My master plan hadn't worked—not at all. Nothing worked. Not my lungs, not my hips, not even my head was working right. Tears—not from pain but an accumulation of physical, mental, and emotional exhaustion—welled up in my eyes. Again, I found myself wishing...praying...willing into existence...peace, quiet. *Please don't ask. Please don't ask. Just smile. It's OK to acknowledge. Just please don't ask. I can't talk. I can't utter a single word.*

It's hard to describe my feelings when I walked into the school office. I looked at the secretary who greeted me with a familiar smile. I was the "room mom" for my boys' classrooms at the time, so her face was as familiar to me as mine was to her. She saw that I was struggling to speak. It was almost as if she could read my mind. Every time I tried to open my mouth, it was like a sea of tears immediately came to my eyes. I couldn't speak. She stood up, alarmed, and asked, *"Can I get the boys for you?"* I took a breath, and my shoulders relaxed as I nodded gratefully to her. She had asked the simple question that I couldn't seem to ask. I didn't want pity or offers of sympathy or support. My ego and my shame simply wanted to escape to a safe place.

Of course, I had to find my words in order to convince my boys I was OK. "Hey guys! I know. Kinda gross, right? It looks way worse than it is. I'm fine. Right? You can tell! Right? Let's get home and get cozy!" Now it was time to walk away from the pseudo-comfortable yet compassionate and supportive environment of the office. With the boys in tow, and my tail between my legs, I head back through the now-much-larger sea of parents by the gate. I heard the voice again—that voice I had ignored when I had first arrived. This time his tone was more assertive, almost aggressive. Almost cringing, I didn't want to even look to see who was talking. He seemed angry with me, which confused me, but I certainly wasn't in a position to hold a coherent and meaningful conversation. Whoever he was...he was definitely speaking directly to me, but this time he felt so uncomfortably close that I sort of cringed and leaned away, squinting and shrugging my shoulder toward my ear as if to protect myself. I could feel his breath on my neck. His voice was deep in tone and full in volume, like a deep whisper, but it carried the power of a shout.

I had been caught.

"Yeah, I'm still here. I've told you...I'm not goin' away...EVER. I'm here, and I'm going to continue to push you until you pay attention. Do I have your attention now? Do I?"

Timidly, awkwardly, I looked around—it became frighteningly clear that this was a message that only I could hear.

The voice continued:

"I promise you, I will take away your body. I will take away your mind if I have to. I will take away everything you love until you've got nothing left to work with but your spirit. THAT is what I need from you. Your spirit. All of it! Do you understand me? You need to do what you're supposed to, which

may not necessarily be what you want to do. It may not be what you think is fun! But you...will...do it."

To this day, I could pinpoint the exact location where I heard this voice. I saw nothing—nobody. Just a clear and present voice. Call it God. Call it the universe. Call it my subconscious. But whoever spoke those words to me clearly possessed the authority to do so and the power to make the message stick.

I don't know what I looked like from the outside, but on the inside I was shocked, horrified, and ashamed. By then, enough time had passed that my injuries and open wounds were growing more inflamed, angrier. I was moving ever more slowly. The after-school hustle and bustle of happy kids and shouting parents had me nearly in a panic. I was afraid that a) one of the elementary school kids might run into my tender road-rash and gauze-covered injuries, but more importantly, I was afraid that b) they'd see me, an adult that many of them had grown to know and love, in a condition that young eyes probably shouldn't see.

As the dizzying sounds and swirling energy from the end of the school day at the busiest pick-up time reached a deafening crescendo, I felt like I might have to find a spot to lie down and call an ambulance. Then, at the precise moment that I had given up, as I started to bend down and lower myself onto the grass next to the busy sidewalk, my friend Curtis grabbed me from behind, almost as if he'd anticipated my collapse. He grabbed my arm and slid his way under my shoulder in an effort to hold me up. I didn't know if I was gonna laugh, cry, or pass out. If memory serves me right, I think I did all three.

This brief but profoundly impactful experience happened about 45 minutes after a 41-mph cycling accident left me unconscious and alone on the side of the road. I was so confused, so scared. I was literally tattered and torn, but I got the message, loud and clear.

The voice? Who was speaking to me on that fateful day? I don't know, but it was someone or something of considerable power—guiding, mentoring, evidently even forcing me to do what I'm supposed to be doing.

And what is it that I'm supposed to be doing? I'm supposed to learn. Digest. Process. Apply what I've absorbed. Simplify what might feel overwhelming or complex or out of reach to others, then make it available to whoever wants to learn and grow. I'm supposed to harvest the insights of those far wiser than I, then make them accessible to all—kids, young adults, anyone interested. It's my calling. My purpose. It's what I'll do... evidently whether I want to or not.

2

What's Really Going on
in this Head of Mine?

This book is a heartfelt recounting of my journey, sharing my personal point of view. This book is also inspired by a quiet but burning desire to help. To shine a light on a few things we know very little about: Emotions, depression, happiness, our brains, our intuition, our senses, our feelings. In an effort to lend some credibility to these thoughts and ideas, I will occasionally share clinical or scientific information I've learned from my own curious wandering, reading, searching and re-searching.

Back in the '90s, after yet another fall from a road racing bike, my neurologists (Dr. Volpe and Dr. Stephens) diagnosed me with something called "Pugilistic Dementia." I didn't know what that meant, but I figured a diagnosis including the word "dementia" probably wasn't a good one.

"Pugil" is a Latin term for boxer; a *pugilist*. *"Dementia,"* although not a single disease in and of itself, is a general term to describe symptoms of

impairment in memory, communication, focus, and thinking. So Pugilistic Dementia was a term used to describe the condition many veteran boxers found themselves dealing with as they aged.

Today, as highlighted by the Will Smith movie *Concussion*, doctors and journalists refer to this condition as CTE or Chronic Traumatic Encephalopathy. **Chronic:** *persisting for a long time or constantly recurring.* **Traumatic:** *relating to or denoting physical injury.* **Encephalopathy:** *widely spread disease of the brain that alters brain function or structure.*

Just writing those phrases incites a palpable fear. Speaking them aloud brings tears to my eyes. There's power in naming something. I do my best not to empower it. But the path outlined in *Concussion* is not a path I care to walk down anytime soon. It's one riddled with constant decline and degradation, the worsening or introduction of depression, and significant emotional pain—all things I've had no shortage of in my seemingly idealistic life already. I don't know if there's room for more.

Now that some time has passed, I can look back and laugh at some things. Although it's not actually funny, humor is a trusty coping tool. I often laugh at instances when I had become a source of great amusement for my friends and coworkers. The closer the friendship, the more laughs they'd have at my expense.

Comments such as, *"Bro! Do you have that $100 I loaned you last month? I kinda need to get that back if that's cool."* This when I had never actually borrowed any money.

Voicemails like, *"Hey man! Where are you? You're supposed to be here by now! We're all waiting on you. Are you good? (long pause) Haha. Just kidding, brother. I hope you're doin' OK! We miss you!"*

And one of my all-time favorite pranks…

Two buddies hung women's clothes in my closet. On its own, that seems pretty harmless. But I didn't have a girlfriend at the time. Imagine the rabbit hole that little prank sent me down when I opened my closet door and saw a bunch of girl's clothes hanging there. I might have stood there wondering for twenty or thirty minutes, waiting for the synapses in my brain to reconnect.

Honestly, remembering it now, this stuff is hilarious. Some of the stunts were legitimately brilliant. But waking up alone to those thoughts was confusing, numbing, humbling, and often humiliating.

To give perspective, think about this for a moment. Humiliation, for all practical purposes, requires others. It just does. It's either caused by others (someone laughing at us, teasing us, even in good humor) or caused by us (by laughing at someone else's misfortune). But to be alone, literally alone and to somehow still feel humiliation? That's a frightening and confusing place to be. It must be similar to someone experiencing an anxiety attack when there's no rationale behind it. It's a place I wouldn't wish on my worst enemy.

3

Chronic Traumatic Encephalopathy

If you're unfamiliar with CTE, keep it on your radar. I'm grateful for the work that doctors, scientists, coroners, psychologists and others continue to put in. More than 300 professional athletes in the NFL have been posthumously diagnosed with CTE. Posthumously—diagnosed after they had already passed!

Dave Duerson (Chicago Bears) died of a self-inflicted gunshot wound to the chest. He left a note to his family that read, *"Please, see that my brain is given to the NFL's brain bank."*

Junior Seau (best known as the backbone of the San Diego Chargers defense) also took his own life. A teammate commented that he knew Seau intentionally shot himself in the chest instead of the head with the hope that experts could examine his brain more closely to learn more about the disease and how its insidious nature can bring even the strongest men in the world to their knees.

On a side note, I find it perplexing that the NFL "team doctors" are the ones who ultimately determine if a player is well enough to take the field. These team doctors' wages (not just pay, their entire compensation package) is paid for by the same team these injured athletes play for. In my opinion, that appears to be a blatant conflict of interest. That would be similar to a doctor employed by Tesla determining if a Tesla employee is well enough to work the assembly line that day. Wouldn't it?

Sports aren't just sports. They aren't just entertainment. Consider this. An estimated value of the Dallas Cowboys alone is over $6 billion. There are 32 NFL teams; each has a stadium, merchandising rights, and countless other revenue streams. Sports are big business, and if key players are on the bench, it immediately impacts the bottom line.

Ryan Freel (MLB), Ty Pozzobon (Rodeo), Rick Rypien (NHL), and countless other professional athletes have taken their own lives, even years after expressing their concerns about depression and CTE.

Selfishly, none of these CTE-related losses hurt me, affected me, and scared me more than learning that a hero of mine (and someone I grew to call a friend as his life drew to a close) had also taken his life. Dave Mira—24-time X Games Medalist, BMX, mountain bike, triathlon, and cycling legend—took his life after losing his long-time battle with depression.

One of the most frustrating aspects of dealing with CTE and memory loss is how serious and seemingly inconsistent the damage can be. The best way I can describe what I've felt so many times is that it would be like reading a 300-page book about your life—or about anything at all—but pages 65 and 66 are gone. So are pages 240-270. You just don't know they're gone. You read. You get confused. You go back. You read again, and nothing makes sense other than the fact that you know that something is missing. Something belongs in those spaces. Then someone asks you about the book, and you're afraid to even open your mouth because you know something's missing, but at the same time, you couldn't possibly know what it is…because it's just gone.

I also didn't know, or at least didn't fully appreciate, how elusive the answers to this memory puzzle can be. Something incredibly ingrained can disappear for an instant, a while...or forever. My old memories are bulletproof thus far. More recent memories, less so. My iPhone is filled with alarms, crutches for my mind. Not so much to wake up for work but reminding me to do the things I look forward to most: "Pick up the kids at school!" or "Go for a run!" At one point in 2021, I had to set alarms to remind me to eat. Looking back now, the scope of what's been going on—what I've been managing—is overwhelming.

4

My Very Own Private Humiliation

The following three instances are just a few of my most memorable reality checks. These reality checks made it a little clearer to me that this simply wasn't gonna get better. It was something I was going to have to live with and something I'd have to watch and manage constantly.

I vividly remember these instances (I know…ironic, isn't it? To remember instances of forgetfulness?) that have stayed with me over the years. These experiences left me running for the comfort and safety of solitude and isolation, a place to set down my fears and humiliation, without judgment from anyone else. A place to close my eyes and let the apparent chaos dissipate like sand through a sieve on the beach. These three experiences clearly pointed out that I could no longer hide or pretend I was OK. Three experiences of being alone in my confusion, too ashamed to ask for help…until I had to.

Hey Turtle! Where's Our Couch? (About three weeks post-accident)

This story is about the time my friends rearranged my furniture while I was sleeping—yes, the same friends who'd put girls' clothing in my closet.

After a particularly hard hit on the head sustained during a road-racing accident at Thunder Hill Park in Northern California, I found myself sleeping a lot. There were a number of injuries, including my head injury, that left my body completely focused on one thing: Healing.

And when I say sleeping 'a lot,' I mean virtually sleeping around the clock upon returning home from the hospital. People must have checked on me, fed me, and ensured I was clean with fresh sheets and pajamas, but to this day, I have no idea who that would have been. If that was you—Thank you.

At the time, I lived with a good buddy I had met in college. We called him Turtle, after a character from a great little surfing movie called *The North Shore*. I remember one particular night when Turtle happened to be at work, bartending at a nightclub in San Francisco's East Bay. I came downstairs to get something to drink. Getting up and down the stairs was still a bit of a challenge with a healing femur, my left arm in a cast, and my right arm in a sling. But I managed. I wedged a large plastic cup into a drawer below the surface of the countertop, rested the orange juice container on the counter, then slowly pulled it over toward me, hopping that the juice would end up in the cup three drawers down, rather than in the drawer or on the floor. Ahhh yes! The sweet taste of victory still resonates. Like the illogical feelings of humiliation I explained earlier, it was odd to feel proud of something so simple...only to look around and notice I was alone. Feeling proud...by myself.

Now with a tall, cold cup of OJ as my companion, my next challenge was the daunting task of getting back upstairs. The oddsmakers would have been wondering...would I get back into bed without a) falling, b) crying in frustration, c) spilling my orange juice all over the carpeted stairway, or d) all of the above, which I had done just a few days earlier.

Standing at the landing, gathering my courage as well as my sense of humor and humility, I felt something odd. Not within me, but something just didn't "seem" right in the house. I couldn't place the sensation, so I ignored it. Then I embarked on my three-minute journey up the stairs. I took one labored step after another...doubting myself, my coordination, and my confused senses. But something still wasn't right in my surroundings. Finally, I stopped climbing the stairs. I very, very, carefully turned around to head back down again. *"Did I leave the refrigerator open...again? Did I leave the burner on...again? I had no food wedged into my sling, so it probably wasn't the stove."* These sorts of thoughts were common and often accompanied me throughout anything and everything I did.

With my shoulder sling supporting my cup of orange juice, and holding the railing with the two free fingers I had sticking out from the cast on my left hand, I carefully navigated the steps back down to the landing. I sat down at the bottom of the stairs, legitimately exhausted, and looked curiously to the right toward the sliding glass door at the back of the house. I squinted my eyes in thought. I wondered. I doubted myself. I waited. I looked to the sliding door again. I wondered again. I waited for the dots to connect themselves, but they didn't. They wouldn't.

Turtle and I lived in a great little condo in Martinez, CA. Albeit a bit of a bachelor pad, it was pretty awesome. The sliding door at the back of the house gave a western-facing view down the valley. The family room on the left, and the dining room on the right, both with large western-facing windows...or so I thought. How is it that I'd lived there for years, but I couldn't be sure how the house was arranged? *"Was the dining room on the left? Hmmm. Lemme think. Maybe I confused my right and my left. Or did I? OK, thinking doesn't seem to be working, so I'll wait some more."* Thus were the internal monologues of my days.

But I wasn't gonna dismiss this feeling. I still felt like something was different, but I couldn't put my finger on it. It was like when I was a young teenager and my dad shaved his mustache off...he looked different, but I couldn't figure out why.

Now 20 years later, sitting on the stairs with a head full of confusion, I finally caved. I couldn't figure it out, so I grabbed the phone to ask for help. I let myself ask someone to connect the dots for me.

I called Turtle in the middle of his busy nightclub bartending shift. Yes...I called him to ask what side of the sliding glass door the couch was on, knowing his smart-ass response would probably be, *"It's on the inside, ya Barney!"* (And yes...in the moment...it did seem like an appropriate thing to do.)

"Hey, Turtle!"

"What's up, Quez?" (Quez [kweez] was a nickname given to my younger brother and I by the Dunlop tire techs at the motorcycle races. Tired of writing "Blasquez" on all of our old tires, they not only shortened it to Quez, but they also butchered the pronunciation...then so did everyone else! Isn't this how nicknames are made?)

"Turtle...You know I'm alright. Right?" Now laughing at myself, *"I mean, I'm a mess, but you're not worried about me. Right?"*

"Ummm...Sure!" He wasn't all that convincing. *"What's up? I'm pretty slammed,"* he politely responded.

"OK. So...(tears of embarrassment and acceptance now filling my eyes) if you're at the bottom of the stairs...looking at the sliding glass door..." I broke down. I could almost see his eyes rolling back in his head, half annoyed but half worried at the same time. *"...is our sofa on the left side of the door or the right side...I mean, as you're looking at it from the inside?"*

There was a long pause, a really long pause. The humiliation grew. I heard the crowd in the background, so I knew we hadn't been disconnected. But he still wasn't responding. He must have been swamped. Then, muffled by his hand, I heard him say to the nightclub manager, *"Hey! Jimmy! Uhhhh. Will you please cover me for a sec? I gotta run home real quick."*

Even writing this brings tears to my eyes. Shame? Sadness? The fact that I had no right to worry others? I can't put it to words, but these moments took...and still take...a big toll.

Before I knew it, in walked Turtle with our buddies Nick and Greg from across the street, all three of them laughing hysterically. I smiled, not only excited simply to see people, as I spent so much time alone, but I was dying to know what was so funny.

Nick and Greg had known that I was a bit of a mess and weren't about to pass up the opportunity to capitalize on that. We were good buddies too, so they didn't hold back. They had come into the house while I was asleep. They moved all the furniture from the dining room into the living room and vice versa. All of it. Not only that, adding to their amusement, they also took all of the food from our refrigerator and our pantry over to their place. Everything but the orange juice—the solitary carton that I hadn't even noticed only 15 minutes earlier. They'd left literally nothing in the fridge but a single carton of orange juice, and it didn't even register with me as odd.

Hey Dude! Where's My Car? (Four months post-accident)

This instance was particularly memorable because it didn't just highlight a legitimately frightening and extended blackout in my memory but also pretty significant impairment of my logic.

I was working as the Marketing Director for Cycle Gear, Inc., a motorcycle apparel and accessories retailer in San Francisco's Bay Area. Every year we had a significant presence at the San Francisco International Motorcycle Show. This event was in November, a full 14 weeks after my road-racing accident. I had been back to work for a couple of weeks at the time, but work was mentally exhausting. The difference between thinking I was ready to work and actually being ready for work was eye-opening, to say the least. I'd show up enthusiastic and grateful to be back in the office—a place I loved to be. But by lunchtime I was feeling anxious. *(I didn't know it was anxiousness that I was feeling until much later—anxiousness that I wasn't going to make it to the finish line that day.)*

Anxiety was another in a long line of new and uncomfortable feelings. The fatigue, the noise, the physical discomfort, the lights; over-stimulation pushed my brain to a pretty uncomfortable place. I didn't simply want to leave; I wanted to hide. I wanted to sleep. Like an infant who hasn't yet developed the ability to differentiate and compartmentalize stimuli, that part of my brain had been injured. Background music, conversations both near and far, the 60-cycle hum of the lights, doors opening and closing, vendors promoting, laugher...it all blended together into a sort of dizzying swirling whirlpool of sensations. The only remedy was peace, quiet, stillness. I had done what I could, putting in about 15 hours on the first day of the motorcycle show. Much more than a typical day, with more and different types of work. With a bruised ego, I was the first to tap out that day, although I knew the Cycle Gear crew was happy I'd hung in there as long as I had. But it was about 10:30pm and definitely time to go.

There were hardly any cars left in the parking lot, which was great for me because I really was physically and emotionally uncomfortable driving, especially at night. As I walked out, I stopped suddenly. "Dude!" I'd only made it fifty yards into the parking lot. *"Where's my car?"* I actually laughed out loud at myself, but the sincere laughter slowly turned to a sort of sadness and acceptance. I remembered that I wasn't really OK.

I must have looked ridiculous, standing perfectly still, mid-stride, in the middle of a nearly empty parking lot, for what had to be twenty or thirty seconds. So, rather than looking like a complete idiot (for longer), I walked back toward the entrance, playing it off as "I must have forgotten something." Well, I had. I had forgotten where I'd parked. But it wasn't the fact that I had forgotten where I had parked that hit me so hard. I had forgotten what kind of car I owned.

I was sitting on the concrete wall near the entrance. This moment and my emotional and mental wellness continued to unravel. I was just fine sitting on the wall, appearing to the world as though I must be waiting for a friend. *"It'll come to me. Any minute, I'll remember what kind of car I drive."* But a moment or two...or ten...later, I had captured the attention of a security guard. *"Hey, buddy! How can I help you?"* Again, I was trapped. I don't lie well, and I was too tired to be clever, self-deprecating, or witty. I came clean. *"Thank you. I'm really embarrassed...I forgot where I parked my car."*

Cue the anxiety. Cue the question...what kind of car did I drive? Cue the humiliation. But tears? Who ordered those?

"I feel you, young man! It's so late. I'm sure you've been here all day long! I'm tuckered myself." I was completely caught off guard by this older man's kindness and sincerity. His name was Buster. I'll never forget it. *"So... whaddya drive? Lemme see if I can't help ya find it!"*

I felt a tear drop down my face. I sat in that moment, present. It was a real moment of surrender. It was humbling, but it brought an unexpected breath of relief. Acceptance. A release of the worries. I was too exhausted to pretend, and it felt pretty good to just let go and let a kind soul hold my proverbial hand in that moment.

After a brief pause, and as that first humiliating tear raced down my face, I had an idea and jumped up like I had won the lottery! Excitedly, I reached into my pocket and pawed through the keys until I found a solitary car key! There was only one car key, and it had a little Toyota logo on it. I literally pumped my clenched fist full of keys into the air and yelled with a smile, *"A Toyota! I drive a Toyota."* And before Buster could ask what kind of Toyota, it all came rushing back. *"Thank you so much! I drive a green Toyota Pre-Runner."*

He rang out on his walkie-talkie, *"Hey y'all! It's Buster. Anyone seen a green Toyota Pre-Runner in one of the parking lots?"* We waited, attentively listening, for a break in the static. The static broke. *"Yep! I've got one in the west lot! It's dark green. It's got a Cycle Gear sticker in the back window."* Buster gestured for me to get into the golf cart. *"Lemme run you over there, buddy!"*

Thank you, Buster.

Perhaps the most thought-provoking part of this entire experience was that although I forgot where I parked (something we've all done countless times) and even what I drove...I still managed to drive myself home. In today's day and age, that's not a noteworthy accomplishment. Getting from point A to point B isn't an earthshattering occurrence. But this was a time before many people had cell phones, and if they did...the cell phones didn't have GPS. Somehow, I remembered how to navigate the streets and highways of San Francisco and the entire East Bay...at night.

The brain is a mysterious thing.

I've shared this story with many people, who often assume, *"Driving home must have been like an unconscious thing! You've driven Bay Area roads and highways for years!"* To which I'd reply, *"Yes, but I had driven my green Toyota for years too…and I forgot that!"*

A Quick Trip to the Office: (Six weeks post-accident)

In addition to teaching, I worked as a realtor. I wasn't a fan of the industry as a whole, but closing a deal or two each year helped keep the lights on and food on the table.

One late morning I went into the real estate office to drop off a document to our escrow team. Not wanting to come off as antisocial, I visited a couple of colleagues, said hi to our broker, and hugged the "den mothers," as we lovingly called the ladies in the front of the office. When it was time to go, I went through the "ready-to-go pat-down." Phone? Yep! Wallet? Yep! Keys? … Um. KEYS? Nope! *"OK, so where are they? Where did I leave them?"* Misplacing keys isn't an experience that's unique only to me. It's something most of us have done countless times. But this time was different.

I made excuses to go back into each of the offices I had visited so I could… *(fill in spontaneously generated reason for the extra visit here)*. I needed to retrace my steps, searching for my keys without looking like I was obviously searching for my keys. *"Hey, Carol! Are we waiting on anything from the buyers' side on the Avenue J deal?"* Nope! No keys. *"Hey, Steve! It was great to see those pictures from your trip to Disneyworld! Say hi to Brian for me!"* Nope…no keys. *"Aimee!!! I'm absolutely loving what your daughter is doing with her plant-based recipes! Tell her I can't wait to try 'em."* Nope…still no keys.

At that point, I headed outside to my truck. Yes, without my keys, because…*(cue the awkward silence)* I forgot that I was looking for my keys. I had already forgotten that I didn't have my keys, and that the whole point of walking around the office for another twenty minutes was to find them. As I reached for the door handle on my truck, still completely clueless that I didn't have my keys, I felt the heat blasting off the asphalt below. My keys were in my truck, in the ignition, with my truck running, where they were when I left them thirty minutes earlier.

At that point I really cowered in fear and shame. Just as every X-ray I had to get read, 'EPX' (Evidence of Prior Fracture), and every new scar seemed to overlap an existing scar, I was now forgetting what I had forgotten.

5

Depression: An Unwelcomed Guest and Its Trusty Companion

"That is all I want in life: for this pain to seem purposeful."
— ELIZABETH WURTZEL

Why, from my earliest memories, did I carry around these insecurities and a deep sadness that ultimately undermined even my best days? Depression has been a close friend of mine during most of my days. But maybe we should call it what it is—an unwelcomed guest.

Mental/emotional challenges, like depression and anxiety come into our lives completely uninvited. They can be brought on by trauma, chemistry, a combination of both...or for seemingly no apparent reason whatsoever. I suffered acutely with depression from my very earliest memories throughout my thirties. Why so much heartache and depression? I can answer that question in three little words: I. Don't. Know. But, like an eerie soundtrack playing throughout the happiest stories of my life and lurking beneath all the blessings, simply put, I felt sad and lonely…a lot.

I almost always felt an ache, a loneliness, a hole in myself somewhere. I couldn't possibly know what others felt, but this sure didn't seem normal, common, or healthy. If it was, apparently, nobody was talking about it. The darkness wasn't just a hole. It was an ugly, cold, and seemingly bottomless hole. It robbed me of the joys that surrounded me. My innate tendency to be empathic made feelings of sadness even more prevalent, more intense, more often. I often found myself walking away from truly happy experiences with a fake smile and an aching heart. It made no sense to me.

As a result of these uncomfortable and occasionally overwhelming feelings, I unconsciously started craving attention from a very young age. Never bad attention, but positive attention, love. Or was it just emotional comfort and safety? I mean, I knew I was loved. I can look back and see it. So maybe there was something inside that just wouldn't let me receive it.

The solution to this particularly tangled web of emotions eluded me for so long. I don't know why I ever felt like that to begin with…I just did.

For me, in the big picture, the cycle and sequence of emotions and actions looked something like this:

1. Feel down for reasons I couldn't understand.
2. Feel even more down.
3. Feel very low for an extended period of time.
4. Experience actual clinical depression.
5. Find an activity that absolutely commands my full and undivided attention so I can stop dwelling in darkness.

6. Find an activity that naturally changes the chemicals in my body (dopamine, endorphins, oxytocin, etc.) rather than ingesting a chemical that changes my mood (benzodiazepine, opiates, marijuana, alcohol, barbiturates, etc.).

7. Hold on for dear life, literally.

8. See #7

9. See #7

10. Breathe.

These mental (and social) attention-grabbing activities seemed like a "healthier" means to an end than relying on prescribed or self-prescribed drugs.

Author, speaker, and mentor, Tony Robbins, often says that mood follows motion. No surprise—he's right. Pushing that idea to the next level, I discovered that the more intense the action and the higher the physical risk inherent in the activity, the better and more prolonged the relief—the better I felt for longer.

Although that's a brilliant solution—albeit temporary—inevitably, the wheels literally and figuratively fall off. In my experience, these "wheels falling off" events routinely resulted in accidents and injuries. Accidents and injuries, in turn, prevented me from taking part in future activities, which was sometimes a hard pill to swallow. Add to that the likelihood that whatever physical trauma I sustained, chasing temporary relief would probably be accompanied by at least some degree of concussion. Psychologically and neurologically, these knocks on the head lead to more frequent and more severe episodes of depression. It was, like most struggles, a slippery slope—or as mom often said, *"You're on thin ice!"*

TBI (Traumatic Brain Injury) and CTE (Chronic Traumatic Encephalopathy) are proven to have a high correlation with depression, suicidal attempts, and sadly, high rates of successful attempts. Mix in the accompanying bone and soft tissue damage as well as the chronic pain that often accompanies it, and you've got the perfect cocktail for disaster. It doesn't take a brain surgeon to see that my "solution" to my sadness and depression was temporary at best, and inevitably perpetuated and even exacerbated those very feelings of sadness and depression.

My temporary "solution" was every bit as ineffective as drugs, alcohol, or any other vice. My brother, a drug and alcohol counselor, offered this bit of wisdom surrounding short-term "solutions" to underlying problems:

"They always took more than they gave."

A depressant like alcohol might temporarily relieve stress, but eventually cause more depression, lethargy, or a hangover. Ultimately, you'll feel lower than you were before. Stimulants like coffee or other forms of caffeine rob from your future energy. While they temporarily increase energy, they eventually bring you down with a crash. Medications often numb us, or "balance us." But we're either bound to them forever, in increasing doses, or when we stop using them, we're in a free-fall, often unable to thrive or even survive without them. For me, these incidents or accidents created a deeper and more desperate search for relief—leading to another catastrophic event, and subsequent deeper and longer episodes of depression.

A couple of side notes on this topic:

1) Why is it that when I discuss this idea with others, inevitably they come to the same default response? The same one they use about fast food, gambling, drinking, recreational drugs use, retail

therapy, etc.? *"Everything in moderation. Right?"* Why do people only ever say that about things that are bad for them?

2) I'm a die-hard vegan. I don't drink. I don't use, nor have I ever used drugs. I don't put anything in my body that I don't think is healthy (except for some non-dairy Ben & Jerry's from time to time). I, to this day, shy away from any medication whatsoever—and I think opioids are the devil incarnate. However, looking back, traditional pain killers may have been an ally instead of a perceived nemesis. They may have provided temporary relief from the pain that was, in turn, worsening my depression. Of course, I'll never know, but a couple of weeks of relief might have been…in fact it was…just what the doctor ordered.

Sorry, Doc.

6

Seeking Attention:
Look Mom! No Hands!

Growing up, I sought attention, admiration, and adoration (which I mistook for love). My seeking often led me to make unwise and often dangerous decisions. I became that stereotypical X-Gen…"X-Games kid" long before the X-Games were a thing.

At seven years of age, I enjoyed one of my first successful "Look, Mom! No hands!" experiences. On September 7th, 1973, on an old dirt levy road on the Sacramento Delta, I did my first one-footed stand-up wheelie on a motorcycle. It was just a little Yamaha GT 80 dirt bike we'd rented from a local dealer, but it was awesome! Back then, people just didn't do the same crazy flips that freestyle motocross stars do today.

That day, my seventh birthday, was the first day I'd ever ridden a motorcycle. With that in mind, consider the lunacy weaving through the following comment: I vividly remember thinking, *If Evel Knievel can do it, I can do it! Right?* It's just the way I was wired. I'm sorry, Mom.

As a kid—heck, even as a young adult—I often found myself looking down a long flight of stairs, or an impossibly steep hill or gap, on a mountain bike, a BMX bike, a motorcycle, or a skateboard, thinking…

"OK!!! Let's do this! This can only go one of two ways: a) I could make it, and everyone will go crazy…again, OR b) I could crash and burn, in which case, everyone will go crazy…again! Either way, I win."

Although I understand now why I did these kinds of things for attention, I certainly didn't understand it then. But looking back it's pretty clear that I was punishing myself for something. I remember instances when the family (often with friends) would go off to do some sort of family activity, but I would make myself stay home, just to deprive myself of the fun. I'd watch ants walk around the dirt in the backyard. I'd go into my room and lie down on my bed—but to ensure that I wasn't comfortable, I'd first take off my sheets, blankets, and pillows. I wouldn't eat because, like most teenagers, I loved food…so I withheld that privilege from myself, too.

It got bad enough at one point during my senior year in high school that I knew things had to change. I overheard my grandfather speaking to my mom during a holiday event. He asked, not knowing I was right around the corner, "Is Andy still skinny, or does he look better now?" My grandpa loved me. I trusted him. He wasn't saying it to make conversation. He cared.

I always had an athletic build, but when depression sets in, it can distort your image of yourself which can lead to a distortion of your physical self.

My "need" for these dangerous and often destructive activities increased in frequency and intensity until I felt like customer-of-the-month at John Muir Medical Center in Walnut Creek. But of course, this was a badge I wore with pride. Really, though—the trauma room nurses and ER doctors, a few of whom I knew on a first-name basis, joked that I'd earned my own parking space right out front! When the broken bones, stitches, and scars were visible, the concern and care of loved ones was there. When the wounds were invisible, lurking on the inside, the support was less evident.

As my friends matured and my family grew tired of my antics, these activities were seen as crazy, even idiotic, instead of courageous. "You're too old to be doing stupid stunts like this!" seemingly played on an endless loop. Stunts like street-luging down Hiller Highlands (just above the Caldecott Tunnel in Berkeley, CA) at three in the morning after all the clubs had closed. Truly stupid antics—stupid enough that even the police didn't want to be troubled. During the wee hours of "just another night of fun" I hopped out of the back of a pickup truck right into the headlights of a Pleasant Hill police car. The truck, unaware, cruised down the steep hill to the pick-up spot. There I was, standing in front of a cop car, at "zero-2:30 hours" dressed in road-racing leathers and a full-faced helmet, holding my Sector 9 longboard. *"Um...Good morning?"* is all I could come up with. After starting to get out of his car, the officer pulled his foot back in, closed his door, and drove away.

I needed to find a new, more socially acceptable way to suffer!

A New Way to Suffer

During my training for the upcoming motorcycle road racing season, a sport that I'm still fanatical about, I discovered an entirely new and "better" kind of suffering: Cycling! I remember thinking, *"Ahhh, yessss! This is perfect. I love it!"* Like an obedient codependent, this means-to-an-end sport came with two huge benefits: 1) Cycling was socially acceptable, so I could pretend that I was "growing up" or maturing and no longer doing those "stupid stunts" anymore, and 2) I was absolutely horrible at it! Really! This was uncharted waters for me. Sucking at a sport, especially a dangerous one, was a new and unpleasant feeling for someone who had never really had to try to be good at sports. It was a next-level type of suffering.

Bring on the pain and humility

In races (and even during training sessions), I was routinely getting destroyed by my competition, off-road and on! Sure, I could bomb down mountains faster than almost anyone, but give me that 12-mile climb up Mt. Diablo halfway through a 45-mile day, and I'd be absolutely wrecked. But "wrecked" was a feeling I had grown to know and love.

This new activity meant that I could have my cake and eat it too! I could, for all intents and purposes, punish myself, and get away with it! There it is: Punish myself. For what? I couldn't possibly understand what, or explain it. In fact, the feelings started when I was so young that the only conclusion I could come close to accepting was that I must have done something dreadful in a past life. It was just something completely out of my realm of comprehension. Regardless, I still felt that I somehow deserved the discomforts; both physical and emotional.

Eventually I started dabbling in cross-country mountain-biking, then downhill cycling. In cross-country (like my performance in the more traditional Tour de France-style road cycling) I was horrible! At my best, I was always in the back half of the field. On occasion, in the back 10%—only once ever getting on the podium, and that was because virtually everyone else quit. But downhill? Downhill was simple. Go as fast as you can! That part I had nailed. I'd been doing that my whole life. (Top speed on a 26" hardtail Specialized M2 Comp: 49.5mph, Sizzler Classic, Mt. Hamilton, San Jose, CA, 1999.) I was competitive right off the bat. So, I did what any other right-minded person would do: I quit participating in downhill events and focused on the suffering.

As "I'm not very good at this!" wasn't a feeling that I was accustomed to, I was really enjoying the newness. "I'm really, sometimes literally, busting my butt day in and day out, and getting nowhere! I'm struggling to be any good at all. No, I'm actually really struggling to simply not be horrible at this sport!"

But, through it all, I carried this faint, seemingly impossible dream in the back of my head. Every now and then, when the noise would settle, I'd flash back to a point in time when I knew I was different...and I accepted it. The Ironman in Kona. It was, and still is, something I always dreamed of. *Maybe someday I'll get myself to Kona and do that Ironman! That's got to be the most beautifully brutal event on the planet.*

Pressing the Rewind Button

"But Dadda...why do you have to do your Ironman races?"

This question was asked of me by my five-year-old son, Jeffrey, just three days prior to my first-ever triathlon. Pondering the question, I found myself in the uncommon position of having no words to adequately respond, especially to a five-year-old. I thought long and hard, but still nothing. It was a good question. Why did I "have to" do this race?

After a few moments I shared the best and most authentic answer I could:

"Little buddy," I told him, "when I was about thirteen or so, I watched the 1982 Ironman Triathlon on TV, and it changed my life forever.

When I was young, our whole family would all get together at your great-grandpa's house for our Sunday brunch. We loved it. Aunts, uncles, cousins, and our grandparents laughed together. We ate good food and played games. My grandpa loved to sit in 'his spot' on the couch, watch golf, eat his brunch, and love the sounds of three generations enjoying each other's company. He loved his family, and he loved watching his golf on Sundays.

"After golf ended, I always heard the theme song for *ABC's Wide World of Sports*! It always sent me running to the TV. *'I wonder what's going to be on,'* I thought. *'Evel Knievel? Car Races? Bobsledding?'* Then I'd hear Jim McKay's voice saying...

'Spanning the globe to bring you the constant variety of sport...the thrill of victory...and the agony of defeat...the human drama of athletic competition...This is ABC's Wide World of Sports!'

"On this particular day there was a new event on called 'Ironman' These people were out of their minds. This endurance race took all day long to finish—ALL DAY! It started in the ocean and ended in the lava fields of Hawaii. But what I remember most from that day, a day that would change my life forever, was not the amazing athletes I was watching. It was not the enormity of the 140.6-mile event. It was the fact that, while I sat at my grandpa's feet, leaning my back against his knees in absolute awe, everyone else seemed almost repulsed by what was unfolding on the TV. Then, with each additional 'ooh' and 'ahh' we uttered, more and more of the family entered the crowded tv room. I was so excited! Something I was immediately completely drawn to...and my family was interested!

"But my enthusiasm and eagerness to share this experience with the ones I loved, the ones I wanted to be proud of me, it all leaked out. The air was pulled from my sails. My family, immediate and extended, kept saying it was crazy. My family kept calling the people competing in the Ironman (not the sport, the people) ridiculous. I even heard someone, an adult I greatly admired, exclaim, 'Oh my goodness! This is just disgusting. What is wrong with these people? Are they sick?'

"We huddled together in a crowded room—my feeling of shame and I. Still leaning against grandpa's knees, the buzzing shock and awe turned to a deafening stillness in my head and in my heart. I was wishing that it was me out there, running through the lava fields. The adult in me wishes that I didn't care if anyone understood it, but I did care. Ironman: I've wanted to do this kind of racing for my whole life, so now...I'm gonna try!"

Looking back at my five-year-old son, I think he'd fallen asleep. I'd probably lost him at *"When I was about thirteen..."*

Later that evening, when the mental noise of raising two boys and working two jobs finally quieted, I realized that a more truthful answer wasn't conveniently sitting on the surface. It was deeper. But how much deeper? I wasn't aware of just how deeply I'd have to dig in order uncover it.

And so began my love/hate relationship with endurance sports.

Triathlon. I trained, I rode, I ran, I swam, I learned about nutrition. Lather. Rinse. Repeat. I completed rides that exceeded the bike leg of the Ironman. Did a couple open-water swims and a couple half-marathons. I was on my way. Then, albeit completely idiotically (noticing a trend here?), I dove in head-first. In 2001 I registered for one of Scott Tinley's triathlons in Santa Barbara. Looking back, I now know that I didn't have a snowball's chance in hell of finishing that race. But, like always, failing would have been an epic adventure in and of itself.

This race wasn't what we call a sprint distance triathlon, or even an Olympic distance race. It was for real! I was so nervous leading up to it. An ocean swim, with waves and currents and "men in gray suits" (a loving and respectful nickname for sharks). As race day neared, I was literally losing sleep. So much could go wrong, but so much could go right. And regardless of my result on that day, it would be a step toward Kona.

So how did my first triathlon go? I couldn't tell you. I never even made it to the starting line. Instead, four weeks prior to the race, I unceremoniously ended my motorcycle road-racing "career." The months immediately following that accident are still a blur. But what I do know is that, in a flash, I was done.

7

Insert My 2nd 100+ mph Motorcycle Road-Racing Accident

I know, I know…I was gonna stop the childish stunts. Right? Maybe just one more time.

Of course, I didn't listen to doctors and neurologists who told me not to race. They had misguided me, my friends, and my family, for years. What did they know, anyway? I wasn't going to listen to my mom and dad, who had already stood bedside at Santa Rosa Memorial Hospital with their youngest son in a coma—the result of a motorcycle roadracing accident. I was gonna do it right!

My superbike race that weekend went really well. Far faster than ever before…and more fun than I'd ever had. But my last race of the day…of my life…not so much. That one ended up in "in the gravel heap."

So, what was the state of my body and mind after falling off my absolutely stunning, new, custom-painted 2001 Suzuki GSXR? Well, I recently stumbled across an e-mail I'd written to Alpinestars, my Italy-based boot sponsor. It very simply read,

Dear Scott,

I wanted to send you and the fine people at the Alpinestars factory a huge and very sincere thank you. "Grazie a tutti! Grazie davvero!" I know you guys care about each of us and the sports we love.

I recently had a pretty big fall. I didn't break my feet.

Thank you.

Saluti, Andy

The subsequent drive to the local medical facility ultimately landed me back at my home away from home, John Muir Hospital. Cleary, I didn't have any idea how severe my injuries were, evidenced by the fact that before I was taken to the hospital, I thought, *"Hey! Let's stop at Granzella's for our traditional post-race dinner celebration with the crew."*

I mean, that's what people do after an accident. Right?

8

That's What People Do. Right?

My brother, my friends, and I had a rich, sincerely heartwarming tradition during race weeks. This post-race tradition really was just as important or more important than the races themselves. We'd work hard all week. We wouldn't sleep well. We wouldn't eat well. Our nerves would be shot and our bank accounts empty. We'd bleed, sweat, cheer, and cry. Then, when it was all over, we'd go to the local bar 'n' grill with those we'd been in the trenches with. Occasionally we'd be lucky enough to be accompanied by our sunburned, horrified, exhausted, and emotional but understanding better-halves. We'd eat, drink, and celebrate that we'd survived another weekend of lunacy. Most of us, anyway. There were occasions when not everyone made it to dinner because... well...not everyone made it.

I remember wincing as we seemed to hit every pothole in the road on the way to the restaurant, thinking, *"Yeah! So what? I crashed. But I did it right! Let's go!!!"* I knew I was pushing it...but I wasn't going to break tradition. Attempts at deep, calming breaths—attempts to compose myself—were interrupted by pretty significant discomfort. *"Clearly, I'm injured, but I'm good. Right? These guys have been through way worse.*

Right? C'mon, Blasquez, just harden up…show up…soak it up. Just be. This is better than any trophy. It's dinner with the boys!"

Don't show me yours. I'm not going to show you mine.

Digressing for a moment, back to that hole; that big, dark, relentless hole…my constant companion. I needed this. I needed this dinnertime, this reward. I needed this experience like I needed air. I knew that a lot of the guys I raced with suffered silently as well. Depression wasn't something we talked about, ever, but I could feel their pain—their sadness; their darkness. I could see it in their faces and more evidently through their behaviors.

Not talking about it was certainly a sort of codependency. I think we all knew that. But not bringing it up, not discussing it, was the sincerest sign of love and respect we could show each other. There was an unwritten rule that we'd be cordial, even sincere, but we'd never push when it came to how one was really doing. We'd cope with things—pain, loss, grief, and depression—with a wry smile that, if tested, would turn to a stifled cry, then immediately into laughter and a big, hearty, exaggerated and forced chuckle.

Personally, I could know that in any given moment that I was OK. But, if you wanted to hang out with me (with us), don't you dare make me utter a single word about what's really going on inside. Typically, a complete emotional collapse lurked just below the surface. The first utterance of a single word regarding how I was (or how any of the other guys were) really feeling was like popping the cork on an expensive bottle of champagne: Most of the contents would end up floating away in the mist or end up as a big mess on the ground. I think we all walked around with the understanding that, *"It's here. You know it. I know it. Can we just get on with the laughter and accept the unspoken love?"*

Not discussing our depression went hand-in-hand with never questioning each other's coping mechanisms. For some it was booze, drugs, or both, while for others it might be girls. Some of us buried ourselves in work only to pop up on race weekends, while I engaged in the silent suffering endurance sports. None of us were really OK, so to point out each other's unhealthy paths would be hypocritical.

This codependence was deeper than just a lack of opening up to each other. It overflowed into the fact that we'd rarely, if ever, visit each other in the hospital. Through the years, as we underwent our individual post-accident ER visits, procedures, surgeries, and post-op physical therapy sessions, it was almost awkward how alone we'd be. We didn't want to accept the fact that we were hurt, but it was much harder to see one of "the boys" in pain. Many of our emotional buckets were full and ready to overflow. Seeing a friend connected to a respirator or in a coma might be too much to handle. We all knew how dangerous "too much to handle" was for each other, so we'd never take it personally if we were in the hospital for a few days or home for weeks without so much as a visit or a call.

On one particular day I remember being wheeled to my truck when the nurse stopped my wheelchair at the elevator. Out walked a close friend and fellow racer wearing an awkward and clearly uncomfortable clavicle brace. As we passed each other, we acknowledged each other, shook our heads with a forced grin, then laughed with...and at...each other. I think these deeply buried emotions came from a very real understanding that our activities were legitimately deadly 'games,' and we didn't want to face our mortality.

Back to dinner after the fall...

It took a few buddies, and more than a few yelps and squeals to get me in and out of the truck, but we made it to dinner. With my racing leathers and undershirt having been cut off by the medics, I no longer possessed "appropriate" attire. But we were a resourceful group, and my brother Tim came to save the day (again).

Tim is basically MacGyver—give him two coconuts and some bailing wire and he'll give you a nuclear reactor. He can do or fix anything. As walked toward me at the entrance of the restaurant, I saw in his eyes sorrow and love. My emotions started to slip. I kept flip-flopping from laughing and shaking my head, which hurt like heck, to fighting back tears, which hurt like heck. I couldn't stand up straight. He truly saw me. Raw. Weak. Scared. Ashamed that I had done it again.

The tears I fought to hold back weren't tears of pain, but tears of truth. I knew that he could read the expression on my face. He knew from experience exactly what I was feeling. *"I know this is not good. What the heck did I do to myself? Why? Again? This is NOT good. I know. But PLEASE don't tell anyone. I'm so sorry I did this to you. I'm SO sorry I did this to you."* That's a lot to read from a simple gaze, but he heard me loud and clear.

Perspective

Flashing back a few years earlier to the time I stood alone in the lobby of Santa Rosa Memorial Hospital. In truth, I wasn't alone at all. I was buried in a sea of friends and fans of my brother. Tim, a championship-winning racer himself, had been Life-Flighted out of Sonoma Raceway after the most unlikely of accidents. I stood tall in that hospital lobby, doing my best to remain stoic, but as a minute turned to twenty, then thirty, then thirty-five, then thirty-six...my concerns grew. My game-face was fading. To no avail I kept asking the clerk in the emergency room how he was doing. *"Excuse me. When may I speak with the doctors, please? What's going on? When can I see him? Where is he? I know he's here. I heard the helicopter landing a while ago. Why can't I see him yet?"*

Then, finally...a door opened. A door that led to a long hallway that led to a maze of more long, mind-numbing, sense-disorienting hallways. I expected a nurse or a doctor or even a growingly frustrated ER clerk to walk out, but out walked a handsome, older, well-dressed man. Disappointed, I moved out of the way to let him pass, but he didn't pass. His polite acknowledgment of my manners became a forever deafening beckoning. He had clearly come to talk to me. I'll never forget his first words.

He said, as if he was ordering a coffee, *"Mr. Blasquez, my name is James. I am the chaplain here at Santa Rosa Memorial Hospital."*

My whole world crashed. My mind stopped. My breath stopped. It was as if everything, all of the air, all of the sounds had somehow been sucked out of the room. *"DON'T SAY IT!"* is all I could think. I couldn't even focus.

Tim had always been my best friend, my roommate, my confidante, my trusty codependent, and my biggest fan. We had lost friends together. We had "been there" for parents who had lost their sons, for wives who had lost their husbands, and hardest of all, to hug the little ones who'd lost their dads. I knew just how real this was. Looking back, I remember feeling that familiar, *"Where's Tim? I don't know what to do now."* He wasn't going to be able to comfort me this time.

The chaplain firmly but gently grabbed me by the shoulders as if he had done this a thousand times.

I said, hastily, *"Cut to the chase. I'm sorry. Please just cut to the chase. I've seen this before. I've been here before,"* as if somehow I was going to one-up the chaplain in terms of remaining poised. I wanted to seem prepared...put together. It's better to be than to seem. Seeming put together

53

wasn't helping. *"Thank you, sir. I saw my brother moving on the tarmac (the asphalt). I heard him screaming over the marshal's radio. I know he's OK, like he's not paralyzed, he's alive."* Then my courage faded again. *"Right? He's alive. Right? Where is he? How is he? When can I see him? May I please see him now?"*

The chaplain calmly, quietly, but with authority said, *"Right now, all I can tell you is that your brother is alive. Right now, in this moment, he's still alive."* If there was any air, noise, or life at all left in the lobby it had surely been exhausted at that point. The chaplain continued, *"What you saw and heard at the racetrack is what we refer to as 'combative behavior.' It's what a body often does before it expires. Your brother Timothy is alive, and he's fighting. Do you want to pray with me?"*

Back to the entrance of Granzella's Restaurant

Yeah. My superhero brother Tim had come to help me this time.

He walked toward me with a roll of duct tape, zip-lock sandwich bags, a big bottle of Advil, and the button-up shirt he was wearing earlier in the day. His fear was compassionately tucked away, necessarily out of sight. He knew from his own experiences that I'd never be able to pull a t-shirt on. My collar bone was clearly broken. I couldn't move either of my arms. But an over-sized button-up would slide nicely up and over my contorted body, leaving me dressed in an outfit that was finally "appropriate," or…if nothing else, sufficient to warrant entry into the restaurant.

After making me semi-presentable for dinner, Tim asked the hostess in the restaurant lobby, *"Excuse me. Yes, thank you. I'm sorry for interrupting. May we please have a table for 8? No…10? Or maybe two or three small tables that we can push together? OH! And…I'm sorry…excuse me. We're also going to need some ice…like a pitcher or two full of ice…right away."*

To that, the hostess said, *"Do you mean ice water? Oh my gosh it's hot today!"*

"No," Tim said with a shake of the head and a smile, *"We need ice...a lot of it...right away...please...and thank you so much."* He then proceeded to fill the zip-lock sandwich bags with ice. Then, with the aid of one of our mechanics and my girlfriend, and that roll of duct tape, he managed to tape several bags of ice to my left hand, right shoulder, right torso, and back.

"OK! Let's eat!"

Here, in no particular order, is the laundry list of injuries sustained by me on that one particular day:

- Left side:
  o Two broken proximal phalanges (fingers)
  o Four metacarpals (hand bones) #5 displaced
  o Broken radius and ulna (wrist)
  o Linear fracture of my left femur (upper leg)
- Right Side:
  o Anterior shoulder dislocation
  o Type 2 shoulder separation
  o Displaced fracture of right clavicle (collarbone)
  o Five rib fractures
    ▪ 2 separations
    ▪ 3 dislocations at spine which affect nerves and shoulder function
- Head/Back/Neck:
  o Complex Grade-3 Concussion

- o Flexion-Distraction Fracture (FDF) of cervical vertebrae C3 & C5
- o Compression fracture of thoracic vertebrae T3 & T5

Clearly my "one more stunt" was one too many.

9

The Shame of (Almost) Getting Caught

Unless you're that singular precious soul on earth who's never done anything wrong...you know what it feels like to screw up. You're doing something wrong (not in alignment) and it doesn't sit right with you, in your gut. But you do it anyway. Then...you get caught, or even "almost" get caught. You know...you're speeding, and you see a police officer behind you with lights on and sirens blaring. Then...she passes right by you. WHEW! You didn't get caught, but you learned your lesson, so you slow your driving habits...for a while.

These "almost caught" moments really helped wake me up. They helped me to stop looking for distractions and temporary comfort so I could start looking for guidance and mental/emotional health.

Side Note: There are a couple of graphic descriptions in this chapter. There aren't here for sensation, sympathy, or pity. They're here in case you want to walk this whole journey with me. The takeaway, if you want to skip forward, is that sometimes we can't see the forest for the trees. Sometimes we think that we're feeling sad or dark or hurt or betrayed without being able to see just how much we're flirting with the edge—the end. (Trigger warning: self-harm)

I Hadn't Cleaned Up

I remember being startled awake one day by the sound of the front door slamming. My roommate Turtle had unexpectedly come home early from a short trip to visit his dad. "Queeeeez!" I heard him shout from downstairs. "What's up, my brother?" Although it was the middle of the afternoon, I was sound asleep. I had absolutely smashed myself on the trails that day and I didn't even know I had fallen asleep until I heard his call.

As I sat up and tried to shake off the brain fog of my nap, I could feel the burn of the day's ride, and maybe a bit of a sunburn too. I had ridden hard earlier that morning on some hot, dusty, and really steep trails. As I began to wake up and come out of the fog, a sense of panic and humiliation began to grow...but why?

I hadn't cleaned up.

As I stood up to go and greet Turtle, I looked down at my legs, which were now oozing a pinkish-clear liquid. My thighs looked as though I had, yet again, bounced down a gravel hillside or maybe hit 'em with a cheese grater. But I hadn't.

I limped as quickly as I could into the bathroom we shared upstairs. I had showered there before I'd crawled into bed to nap. There, on the floor, I saw the remnants of what had become an increasingly normal occurrence for me. There sat the most unlikely group of items you'd ever find on a bathroom floor: My mountain bike shorts were next to the shower along with my jersey and my cycling socks—all of which were absolutely filthy. My 14-inch diver's knife was on the counter, and a wad of bloody tissue had evidently missed the wastebasket where I had un-successfully thrown it. There were smudges of blood on the vanity and several large drops on the floor and on the toilet lid. Only in hindsight can I see just what a terrifying mess the bathroom was. Only looking back could I put myself in a position to think about how Turtle might have felt, had he innocently walked into a less than innocent setting. Looking down at my thighs, it wasn't a sunburn that ached so acutely, but a carefully engineered, self-inflicted "cycling accident."

When you ride and race hard, it happens. You fall. It sucks…or so they say. But this left me with countless opportunities to plan out my next premeditated "wreck." After riding, I'd place the blade of the dive knife, serrated side down, on my thigh—at the precise point where the elastic band at the bottom of my cycling kit met my skin. Then, with a force sufficient to draw blood, I would drag the blade's edge down my thigh. This gave the illusion that the "road rash" started at the point where my skin wasn't protected by my cycling kit. If I started with quite a bit of pressure, then lightened the pressure of the serrations as I dragged the blade down my leg, it would create a very authentic-looking wound. Then, like a Hollywood special effects artist, I would doctor up my new wound to give it a more believable appearance. Turning the blade over and repeating the process a dozen or more times, it created a more broad and shallow abrasion. The combination of both sides of the knife and mastering the art of recreation led to some pretty remarkable samples of 'faux road rash'!

On this particular day, I had made a mistake. The serrations on the blade of a knife are symmetric—perfectly spaced and man-made. Gravel isn't. So I would occasionally have to create additional cuts that were roughly parallel, but not perfectly parallel, to the existing cuts. But that day's cuts went too deep. It didn't take much to accidentally overstep the boundaries that even I had set for myself. This unintended laceration likely added to the depth and length of my afternoon slumber.

It's ironic, isn't it? That simply exchanging one pain for another brought even a modicum of relief. The often-excruciating pain of the blade, or a broken piece of glass, literally felt like taking a pain killer. I thought, for years, that it legitimately allowed the pain in my heart to peacefully flow out of me. I knew that physical wounds would heal, but it was harder to visualize the emotional wounds—and I still hadn't found a way to heal them or find relief.

At that point in my life, I gladly chose what I considered the lesser of all evils. It took decades before I'd realize that my emotional pain wasn't peacefully flowing out, or even subsiding. It was simply being drowned out by the noise of physical pain that I preferred to feel, almost like turning up the radio in your car so you no longer hear the clunking sound it's making.

Although most of my self-inflicted physical wounds didn't leave substantial scars—physical ones, anyway—it wasn't long before I started recognizing that I no longer had untracked skin to use as a canvas. So bigger scars would hide smaller ones, and new scars hid the old. I was soon known as the craziest mountain biker around. If they only knew the truth, my cover would have been blown. But, as with motorcycle road racing, I lived with the motto, "Always ride over your head!" With that, a little wit, and some creativity, I could hide anything.

Hey! Hey! Hey! It's OK!

In a similar way, and with the same peaceful reprieve from emotional pain, I nearly gave it all away one night at work—all of it. Yes, while I was at work. Somehow with my wits about me, I managed to elude my doubters yet again, but that was as close as I ever got to blowing my cover.

As a motorcycle and bicycle racer, I spent my winter and early spring months completely sober. As a bartender, it wasn't fun, but it was necessary. So, from January 1ˢᵗ until the Sunday night after our first race, my brother and I wouldn't drink a drop. Looking back, I'm surprised that this memorable night unfolded the way it did when I truly had a completely clear and peaceful mind.

I had become an expert at hiding not just my physical wounds, but my depression as well. I could be the life of the party, the funny guy, the crazy guy who'd be the first one to try the next stupid stunt. I was the one who would listen intently and the guy who really cared about the heartaches of others; but at the same time, I'd feel completely buried in emptiness. Is that a thing? Buried in emptiness?

The comparison of my "life-of-the-party" persona no longer wanting "to be" might have seemed like a pretty big jump to an outsider. But on the inside, it was a much shorter journey. I was often just one thought away from calling it a day. Sometimes it wasn't even emotional pain that led to these self-injury coping episodes. On that particular night at work, I actually felt pretty happy. That feeling of happiness brought strength and a smile. That strength in turn brought confidence and a bit of peace. But it was that confidence that almost caught me out.

Running from the bar to the walk-in cooler, I grabbed another case of Coors Light, then spun around to run back to the bar and dive back into a busy nightclub atmosphere. But I hit the shelf in the cooler when I spun around and broke a bunch of bottles. Beer sprayed and leaked all over the floor. I knew that the bar was slammed so I couldn't do a thorough clean-up at that moment. I'd have to clean it up after we closed. But not wanting anyone to get hurt, I started to just pick up the big pieces of glass and sweep the smaller pieces to the side until I could take care of it later.

Without a single second passing, I reached down with my right hand and grabbed the top half of a broken beer bottle. I, without hesitation or thought, walked to the shelf that I had bumped into just a moment earlier. I made a fist with my left hand, then placed my arm on the shelf to stabilize it, wrist side up. Without a second thought, I used the broken bottle to slice a really long and deep cut into my left wrist. Not perpendicular to my arm (not the dramatic way you'd see in the movies), but diagonal, nearly parallel with my forearm. I did it the way you'd do it... if you really meant to.

Then, just as my roommate had almost caught me bleeding in the bathroom, I heard the door to the walk-in open. "Oh, god! What a mess," I heard from one of the servers as she opened the door. My heart froze. She gave me a look that said, *"Oh man! That sucks."* Thankfully, though, she was referring to the broken case of beer strewn across the walk-in cooler. I thought, *"Whew! I thought I was caught for sure!"* Then she finally, truly saw me.

I will never forget her uncontrolled and horrified scream, becoming more and more hysterical She dropped everything in her hands in a panic. Money and tickets and credit cards were all over the beer-soaked floor. I remember running after her to comfort her and assure her that I was OK. *"Hey! Hey! It's OK...I'm OK."* I was yelling. *"I accidentally dropped a case of beer and I broke a few bottles. One cut my arm, but it's OK. I'm fine! Look, I'm fine!"*

I will never forget the deepest and most sincere feeling of sorrow that immediately overcame me—sorrow that I feel deeply to this day, as I write this with tears in my eyes as I think about the panic I caused for those around me. People saw the server screaming, they saw me, they saw blood. They thought that she might have been hurt, because I was doing all I could to comfort her. She was repulsed by me and recoiled each time I tried to approach her to provide any kind of comfort.

While the club owner tended to my cut, which was deep enough to see the fat and connective tissues within my arm, I was lost in my thoughts (and probably shock).

"What the hell!!! GODDAMNIT! You have no right to ever, ever make someone feel like that. NEVER! How are you ever going to help to her un-see what she just saw? You can't! You HAVE TO STOP…RIGHT NOW!"

I want to say that was my last episode of intentionally hurting myself, but it wasn't. I still bear the scars of later instances, but eventually the shame overwhelmed my search for relief, so I stopped. Although, on the surface, it appeared to be another failed attempt at finding peace, it wasn't. The path to finding peace is littered with failed attempts, with each subsequent failure leading me in the right direction.

10

The Start of a New Challenge

Please forgive the dark backstory. Unfortunately, I'm sure some of you have walked a similar path...and I'm sorry. I'm so very sorry.

As the physical and emotional scars left no room for more suffering...I stopped. Just another morning. Another morning. Another morning...until I sat in bed one morning, absent the will to get up again... wondering if significant feelings of discomfort were just going to be a part of my life forever. In came the uninvited "guest."

"This is what you want. Isn't it? A challenge? Now let's see you get to Kona, tough guy! Are you going to grow up now? Are you going to show me what you're made of? Are you going to accept yourself for who you are, or are you going to continue to squander your gifts and sabotage your happiness... your own life? What's it gonna be, huh? It's up to you!"

I found myself at the start of a huge new challenge: Healing.

Fast forward a couple of years. I'm running again, cycling and swimming too! My shoulder didn't handle the workload with a smile, so we had it fixed. Re-stabilization surgery, SLAP repair, rotator cuff, tendon debridement, etc. Good as new. Let's keep rolling.

A couple of years later, now with kids in tow, I'm still trying to find a fraction of my former self. I ran myself into the ground, requiring Achilles tendon replacement. 'Two steps forward and one step back' never rang so true. But this time, with wisdom and continued growth. This time it's with the support and coaching I receive from my MaccaX (a Sydney-based triathlon club) teammates, and the support of my biggest fans—my boys.

At this point, in my 50s, I not only have a purpose, but a duty to model living rightly. I have the two most precious boys on Earth, and I'd be devastated to have them live the life that I chose to live.

As for these triathlons and endurance sports, it was no longer about the medals or the bragging rights. The truth is that the training, the pushing through, the breaking down of barriers, the dissolution and subsiding of the ego, the discipline it takes and the will to keep going no matter what…that makes me a better person. The alone time on long runs, the loneliness of long solo rides, and the quiet, mind-numbing hours staring at the black line at the bottom of the pool have made me—and continue to make me—a better man. I guess that's the allure now, and the longer-term goal.

There's still suffering. But now it's legitimate. It's purposeful. It forces me into places where my ego can't survive. It strips me down. It forces me to be raw and authentic with myself—to be authentic, to be "me," whatever that means. Triathlon has become so important to me. The personal pilgrimage is constant, and I like it that way. It provides a time and place for me to dump my stresses and heal a little more. In a funny way, it lets me stand taller because my training helps me find peace; or rather, it helps me create it. My aim is not to stand taller than someone else, but taller than I did yesterday.

Bek and Siri (Team Sirious Tri Club) helped me find peace in my training. Grace and acceptance. Humility and happiness. The events are no longer about the events. I never stand proud because I finished an event. It's not for the medal around my neck. There are more valuable medals! It's about the journey and who I'm becoming along the way.

11

The Long Climb Out

How did I get out of the darkness, the sadness, the mess…and why did I even bother?

Love. Real love.

I knew what "love" was. It made me smile. It made me cry. It made me daydream. I read about it in books. I watched it on TV. I hid my tears when I cried watching movies about "true" love. Yes, I was that one guy that actually loved *The Notebook*. I loved everything about love.

But I watched *Star Wars* too. I watched *James Bond*, and *Nightmare on Elm Street* too. They entertained me, inspired me, and scared me… but I also knew on every level that they were purely fictional. Love—like wizards and superheroes—was designed, created, and published in order to illicit emotions within us. To sell tickets and cable subscriptions and books. That's what love is. Right? It's a room full of writers, producers, and directors collaborating to find ways to stir our emotions and dreams. It's a means to a profitable end while providing a service to all those in the market for that type of experience. Some people like action movies, horror films, or comedies. Others like love stories. To me, "love" was very much the same. A genre. A purely fictional thing. I loved "love" like kids love Disney!

Man, I wanted it so badly. I wanted to feel love, and even more so I wanted to give that feeling to someone else. I wanted to give love. I wanted a place to rest my head—a place where I felt loved, cared for, comforted. But I also wanted to meet Santa and the Easter Bunny when I was young. I remember, with my tail between my legs, as subtly as ever, asking for love. What a shameful feeling it was: to need. And the shame was heightened with every rejection, until I traded my desire for love for an absence of disappointment and shame—and that didn't happen either. Unless you counted meeting Santa at a dozen malls. Clearly, he wasn't real; nor was love.

Then, one day in October of 1999, it was as if Santa himself landed on my roof. I saw love. Real love. Not at a wedding. Not at a birthday celebration. It wasn't even between a man and a woman, but between a father and a son. It was in the lava fields of Kailua-Kona, Hawaii. It hit me so squarely in the face that, looking back, I quite literally owe everything in my life after October of 1999 to Dick and Ricky Hoyt.

I could fill the remaining pages of this book with the stories and accomplishments of Team Hoyt, but I'm sure someone's already done that. Although it feels like a bit of a disservice to abbreviate their impact on me, in the spirit of brevity, here's what I remember from that warm October afternoon.

A strong, loving father, a father that wasn't going to put his son (born with severe cerebral palsy) in an assisted living facility as doctors advised...he simply loved his son for one more day: One long, difficult, beautiful, life-changing day.

Dick Hoyt put his adult son Ricky in a small zodiac boat that was tied to a rope. The rope was tied to a harness that Dick was wearing. Ricky, covered in sunscreen, sunglasses, a life vest, and a ball cap, was ready to start Ironman Hawaii. They'd do it together: A 2.4-mile swim. A 112-mile bike ride on an old, heavy, custom-built tandem-style bicycle. A 26.2-mile marathon, where dad would push his son to the finish line.

Due to mechanical issues, the race didn't go as planned. They didn't make the bike-to-run cutoff in time. But Ricky wanted to keep going anyway, so Dick put his son in a wheelchair and pushed him for 26.2 miles. They finished just before the 17-hour cutoff.

That day, a father and a son chose to spend 17 straight hours together. When's the last time you heard of that? It was love. When Dick was asked, *"Why do you do this? It's clearly not something people do!"* Dick, with tears in his eyes, said that Ricky didn't feel handicapped when they were racing. What father wouldn't do this for his son? Then...Ricky's answer to a similar question sewed it up for me:

From an interview with Dick Hoyt:

"If Ricky was physically able to do something he'd probably play basketball, football, or hockey. But then he always says,

> *'No. The first thing I'd do is have you sit down in my wheelchair, and I'd push you.'"*

That was it.

It was love.

They weren't actors. They were real. That meant that love was real.

I had hope.

Hope was my seed.

12

Hope Is the Seed

Hope is the seed. Opportunity is the soil. What we do with our opportunities determines how our flowers bloom.

As a single dad, how was I going to find/make opportunities in a schedule to tend to my soil? I had to make changes. I had to break old habits that didn't serve me—old paradigms, old perspectives. But how?

I remember Tony Robbins talking about "NET Time:" No Extra Time. How can I add what I need to add (learning, growing, forgiving, healing, breathing) into a schedule that's completely packed already? Well, it was easier than I expected. It was amazing how much time I spent "on autopilot." I'd be folding laundry, driving, doing the dishes, exercising, etc.—all things that needed to be done, but I could watch, listen, and learn at the same time! So I started listening to audio books and podcasts.

My first effort was incredibly memorable. One of my buddies from motorcycle racing was getting married. We were all gonna meet up in Vegas. I remember dropping off a few buddies at the Oakland airport. Then I got back into my car, hit a gas station on the way out to grab a huge Diet Coke and some sunflower seeds. With the windows down, and hope as the seed, I took the opportunity to drive instead of flying to Vegas, and I used that opportunity to listen to my first audio book.

I had absolutely no idea where to start. I remember my ex-wife watched *Dr. Phil* a lot. I remember him listening to his guests justifying their behaviors, defending themselves, to which he'd say, *"Yeah! And how's that workin' out for ya?"* I LOVED that! I'd listen to the folks trying to justify their individual dysfunctions and think to myself, *"Man! Do you want to be right? Or do you want to be happy!"* (No kidding. That was something I later heard on the *Dr. Phil* show). Long story short, I went to the library and checked out two audio books: Dr. Phil's *Getting Real* and *Learn Italian in Your Car*. I never got to the second book.

I got to Vegas. Met the guys for drinks, then headed to the Supercross Finale at Sam Boyd Stadium. And like the true partiers that we were, after the race we went to a friend's house and ate frozen pizza and watched the new *Planet Earth* in HD (yes, HD was still a thing)!

With the ideas and perspectives, the thoughts and practices outlined in *Getting Real*, I got in the car to head home. Time to learn Italian. Right? Nope! I drove to Barnes & Noble in Las Vegas and bought Stephen Covey's *7 Habits of Highly Effective People*. Not only were the perspectives plentiful and helpful, they were principle-centered. They were timeless. But almost as important as that...the book referred to countless other authors, leaders, and philosophers.

Deepak Chopra, Dr. Wayne Dyer, Gandhi, Eckhart Tolle, Laozi, Marcus Aurelius, Viktor Frankl, Dr. Martin Luther King Jr., Tim Ferriss, Robert Kiyosaki, Napoleon Hill, the Heath brothers, and on and on and on.

I'd read (listened to) one, then another, then a third. Then I'd forget something. I'd go back to the second book and listen to it again. I'd hear something I didn't hear before—or, even more common, I'd hear something that I had heard before which I thought I understood but now saw differently...like I had heard it for the first time.

Books led to podcasts which led to TED Talks and seminars and groups on social media platforms. This paradigm-changing, healthy, exciting and engaging habit started in 2007 and it hasn't slowed a bit. I digest things a bit more deeply today than I did back then, but I'm still learning. I rest my mind between books now; rather than leaning on these mentors and coaches and sages to literally save my life, I use them to guide it.

The following ideas are really just the tip of the iceberg in terms of what I've learned that keeps my heart peaceful, my mind calm, and my life happy, regardless of my circumstances:

- You can literally, neurologically exercise happiness in the same way you can exercise your muscles.

- Forgiving others is about us, not them. Without forgiveness, we're left with resentment and pain.

- Forgiving ourselves makes room within us to receive what we've been missing for so long.

- "Resentment is like drinking poison and then hoping it will kill your enemies." ~ Nelson Mandela

- "The only safe and sure way to destroy your enemy is to make him your friend." ~ Mark Twain

- My parents couldn't possibly have known what was best for me.

- Independence is simply a step toward a greater good—intercedence.

- Equality and equity are very different.
- Stop looking where you fell. Instead, look where you tripped.
- Good decisions come from experience. Experience often comes from bad decisions.
- "We cannot solve our problems with the same thinking we used when we created them." ~ Albert Einstein
- Love, the noun, is the fruit of love, the verb.

13

Why "It's Dad"? Why Now?

I started the "#itsdad" project shortly after the accident and the ominous experience with the voice. As the days passed post-accident, I became increasingly frightened. I simply wasn't OK. I didn't feel invincible. I felt fragile. Timid. For a guy who's not typically afraid of much (periodically referred to as "too stupid to get hurt!"), this clear and present feeling of fear had my undivided attention. Everything that wasn't critical in my life or the lives of my boys quickly faded into insignificance as I struggled to come to grips with how, and sometimes even where, I was at any given moment.

I struggled acutely with short-term memory. I couldn't focus. I found myself in the familiar grasp of feeling extremely uncomfortable in crowded or noisy places. Over-stimulated. Always accompanied by an anxious sadness and an irrational fear. Among friends and family, I buried myself in self-deprecating comments in an effort to make light of embarrassing situations that, at the time, were seriously interrupting my life. Perhaps for self-preservation purposes, I started isolating myself. I stopped accepting invitations. I spent my alone time tuning out the noises of the day, then consciously replacing them with thoughts of my life circumstance. I kept thinking, *"What happens if I lose it all? Everything I've learned? I'm not done being 'Dadda'* (an affectionate term my boys called me when they were young). *How do I share what I've learned, or at least what I can remember, with my boys? It's like a sinking ship. Each moment I wait it gets worse."*

I had a constant and overwhelming feeling that I was (not figuratively but very literally) losing my mind. That last "little tip-over" (a light-hearted euphemism for a severe fall from a bicycle or motorcycle) resulted in my 15th loss of consciousness. How long was I out this time? I don't know. I had been riding alone, training for Challenge Roth, a triathlon in Germany to which I was graciously gifted entry by two-time Ironman World Champion Chris "Macca" McCormack. What I do know is that when it comes to head injuries, 15 is not an insignificant number. This wasn't 15 concussions. This was 15 instances of loss of consciousness...that I can remember. Clearly, this isn't normal. Not every banker, teacher, or mechanic goes through things like this. Right? Or do they? Am I just being soft? As my Aussie friends might say, "Did I just need to HTFU (harden the %#*! up)?"

And why so many knocks on the head? Seriously!? There are good reasons why most folks don't deal with things like this. So why had I had so many? Well, primarily due to...no, *entirely due to* a long history of making some pretty reckless choices. Climbing. Jumping. Scuba diving. Skydiving. Racing anything and everything that required a helmet, and better yet, a fire-suit or road-racing leathers! Any way that I could tempt fate would do the trick.

Although I wasn't aware in those moments, those reckless choices served as a means to an end. They put me into situations that commanded absolute focus and presence. When you're fully present, you're no longer stuck regretting the past or fearing the future. Presence keeps us in the moment; in the now. Being in the moment keeps you from your thoughts and feelings. And other than turning to drugs, alcohol, or women, I would do just about anything to run and hide from any and all of my thoughts and feelings.

During the days and weeks after my accident, as my physical and mental struggles became more evident, I started to really feel that the end was near. I wasn't going to die. Instead, I'd endure something more challenging than death. I was going to live. It sure felt like I would ride the slippery slope toward dementia, but I would be doing it with the complete, painful, and humiliating awareness that it was happening… and that it was my fault.

"But I'm the father of two of the most beautiful boys I've ever seen." I remember really struggling and thinking, *"I can't start fading already! I can't 'not be here' for the boys! Where will they go? They're gonna miss me, and that's not all!!! Who's gonna teach 'em about life? About what matters? OK, OK, OK."*

Feeling deeply alone, pleading, with tears streaming down my cheeks, I must have sounded like an addict fighting for his life…

"For real, this is my last time. I promise. No more risks! Lock me in the house forever…I don't care. Just don't let this be the beginning of the end. I don't care about myself. I can be done. It's OK. I get it. I deserve it. But please, my boys deserve to have a healthy and loving dad, at least through their most formative years. Please…at least let me get through these next few years with my wits intact, then you can take me…or at least my mind. Whatever is right."

I started to feel and fear that there was a time coming in the very near future when I would literally not be able to care for myself, much less my boys. In all truth, I could make peace with that—shameful peace, if there is such a thing, but peace, nonetheless. But since the birth of my boys, my highest priority has always been to raise them with a healthy mindset and a strong yet compassionate heart. As Brené Brown so beautifully penned, *"Soft front. Strong back. Wild heart."*

I needed to model this lifestyle for them. I needed to talk with them, to walk with them, to show them how to navigate life with a sincere smile. This was something I hadn't accomplished in my youth, but I had really mastered in recent years. So if I could help alleviate in them some of the feelings that I wrestled with throughout my childhood, perhaps they'd go on to bigger and better-- and—more importantly—happier times.

As my days rolled by, and I wandered haphazardly through my daily chores and responsibilities, fractured and fragmented life lessons started darting through my mind. Imagine an electrical short that connects for a brief moment, only to cut out a fraction of a second later. The lessons I had learned weeks, months, or decades earlier would pop in unexpectedly and fade away just as quickly as they'd arrived. But when they disappeared, were they really gone? Would they come back? I had little faith that they would. The culmination of my life's learnings and lessons, everything I would pass down to my sons…was fading rapidly. It scared me. It broke my heart.

I literally thought that all of these thoughts would never come back, so when they made themselves known, I'd grab my phone, my laptop, a sticky note, or even a scrap of cardboard so I could capture every shred of memory before these fleeting ideas could escape. I'd text myself a voice message or even record myself trying to make sense of things in hopes that when I watched the video later, it might encourage the synapses in my head to reach toward each other one last time and reconnect.

I used any means possible to hold onto what I could. It was like trying to catch shooting stars with a butterfly net, or maybe something like a tracker hunting its prey, holding on to just the faintest scent of what was just there. *"There's one! Ahhhhh, yesss!!! Gotcha!"* Then, when I had more coherent moments, and as time allowed, I would sit down and look through my notes and text messages. I'd unpack my thoughts on whatever I had briefly captured. I'd share this lesson or that, an experience I'd been through, what it taught me, or lessons that I had learned from my mom, my dad, or the sea of books and mentors I had relied on to help me navigate my own journey.

To this day, I have visions of my boys reading these "It's Dad" letters when they were older. They might reach for them when they grew old enough to benefit from them, even reading them to their own kids someday.

Over time, these memories...their remnants and scraps...turned into memos, then into e-mails I'd send to myself. Some started as social media posts, then turned into blog posts. For the longest time, they were sort of scattered about and in no coherent structure. So, I thought it was time to wrap them up together in a way that would not only be pleasant to read and learn from, but easy to remember and to pass on.

Every note, every blog, and every post is a sincere (albeit virtual) heart-to-heart chat with my boys. Each entry starts precisely the same way...

...imagining them...

...someday or some way without me...

...reading and learning...

...growing, and eventually sharing...

…passing on what mattered most to a friend in need, or even to their own kids.

Each entry starts with, "Hey guys! It's Dad!"

"We shall not cease from exploration
And the end of all our exploring
Will be to arrive where we started
And know the place for the first time."
– T. S. ELIOT

Part 2: Share

The "It's Dad" Blogs

14

Tell Her that She's Beautiful
(The one that started it all)

Hi guys. It's Dad.

An idea crossed my mind this morning after I dropped you off at school. It's bugged me for a while, so I want to work through it and share it with you.

Don't let anybody or anything tell you what is beautiful. A car. A sunset. A person. A poem. It's beautiful because you see it that way. Don't give away that privilege, that power, that freedom, that gift.

We live in a beautiful country. I'm grateful for that, but this is one area where I think America has got it all wrong.

TV, movies, magazines—and, most of all, social media—are constantly telling us what's important, who's cool, and who's beautiful. They (the media, and what we refer to as "opinion leaders") do this because they make money. They make money because we believe them. Think about that for a moment. We let people tell us our own opinions. But doesn't that make our opinions the same as theirs. We like this particular rap artist or that brand and style of shoes; we like this sports team or that actress because they (the influencers, the opinion leaders) tell us to. Directly or indirectly, they guide us.

But hold on. Don't you have your own opinions already? Weren't you born with them? Haven't you developed them as you've grown? Whatever or whoever you're attracted to is your own opinion...not the opinion of your friends, or of society. How can you explain what you find beautiful? You just know! It might be a horse or a waterfall. It might be a guitar or a sunset. It might be a handsome man or a pretty young lady. Beauty is natural, so don't look to magazine covers to see what's beautiful. Don't watch reality TV. Don't see what's being sold to you as beautiful. See what's truly beautiful to you.

As I run through the trails in the springtime, this idea keeps resonating. Do you know the difference between a flowering weed and a flowering plant? I don't. They're green...and they have pretty flowers. Is it a wildflower? Does it even matter if it's a weed or a plant or a wildflower? They're all plants, and they all grow flowers. Right?

But which one is more beautiful? If you ask the florist, he'll tell you that the expensive one is more beautiful, because that serves him. To me, personally, the little wildflowers that line the single-track trails in the Crafton Hills trails are way prettier. They're just there. They are resilient. They live through 115-degree heat and they live through snow. They bloom with the sunrise and go to bed with the sunset...whether we see them or not. That's absolutely beautiful to me. How could a florist, or anyone else for that matter, possibly know what's beautiful to me or to you?

Guys, when you grow just a little older and you find a young lady that you're really attracted to, tell her and show her that she's beautiful exactly as she is...naturally. If she's American, she's probably already thought at one time (or many) that she's not. Sadly, part of the $150 billion we spend on advertising each year in the US is spent convincing young women that they are too short or too tall or too curvy or not curvy enough or that their hair is too curly or too straight or the wrong color.

So…as gentlemen, let's remind them just how wrong the red carpet and magazine covers are. She doesn't need to change her hair, or her skin, or her outfit. She's beautiful just the way she is. If she wasn't, you wouldn't have been attracted to her in the first place, right? But you were…and you are. You're attracted to who she is…how she is.

Is it her intelligence or her kindness that you're attracted to? Is it her strong spirit or her sense of humor? Is it her humility or her confidence? Or is it a unique blend of all of those qualities that she holds? Something attracted you to her, and her to you; something beautiful, and nobody had to tell you what it was.

Sure, when you're out on a date and her hair is just right and her makeup looks great—oh, and she's wearing that cute outfit that you like so much—she looks beautiful! In those times, it natural and easy to say, "Wow! You look amazing tonight!" Of course! But what about when she goes to sleep? What about when her makeup comes off? What about when she wakes up in the morning with messy hair and wrinkly ol' pajamas? Is she still beautiful? Did the beauty somehow leave her in the middle of the night like Cinderella's carriage? Did she somehow, while you slept, become a different person or become less attractive? Of course not.

She is the same person, with the same heart, the same mind, the same sense of humor, the same stubbornness that makes you laugh…and she has the same beauty. It's the truth. I promise. If fact, if you really look at her deeply in those messy-hair, no-makeup, sleepy-eyed moments, she's more beautiful than ever. Let me tell you why.

In those gray-sweatpants moments, those cranky moments of exhaustion, and those red-nosed moments when she's not feeling well… there's real beauty. It's a special, authentic, and precious beauty. In those moments, she is unmasked. She's not pretending. She is her true self. She is letting you in, showing you her genuine self, and that means that she trusts you. She trusts you with her heart and feels safe when she's with you. She doesn't have to pretend to be happy. She doesn't have to "be at her best" every moment, because she knows that she can be herself with you…and what could be more beautiful than that?

So, in those types of moments—when she's tired, sick, disappointed—remind her that she's beautiful, and tell her why. Remind her that she's smart, or maybe that she makes you laugh. Maybe she inspires you to be a better you. Maybe she believes in you and challenges you to become a stronger man. Maybe when she touches you, or she leans on your shoulder, even if just for a moment, the weight of the world melts away. Whatever it is…reminder her that she is precious to you and that she is beautiful.

Maybe she's tall. Maybe she's not. Maybe she's curvy, or maybe she's not. Maybe her skin is dark, or maybe it's light. But one thing's for sure. Her eyes are uniquely hers. There aren't any other eyes like hers, and as she ages…those eyes never will. Her hair is perfect; straight or curly; long or short; blonde, brown, red, or gray. It's perfect. She's perfect.

In the very beginning, be drawn to your partner for who she really is, and that will stand the test of time. We all age. Our skin loses its elasticity. We gain weight. We go bald. We get sick. Through illness or accident, we may even become disfigured. Our bodies change, and there's no way around that. Of course, we're attracted to physical beauty. We're human beings! But *only* being attached to someone because they're "cute" will surely lead to broken hearts down the road if there's nothing inside to support it.

Our outward beauty is something that will always leave us. It's something that we don't ever actually own. We just borrow it, and someday we'll have to give it back. So don't grow too attached to it. Cherish it. Enjoy it. But don't depend on it. Don't tie your happiness to it. It's about heart and character and respect and admiration and joy.

And remember this, guys. A woman's body also changes when she gives birth to your children. That's the way God made it! But on TV, in movies, magazines, and on social media, these changes are criticized, sending young women running to surgeons to get those changes "fixed." It breaks my heart. Those changes should be embraced, revered, and respected—not shamed, hidden, and erased. Those changes are proof of the sacrifice she made in order to bring life into this world and into your lives. Now THAT is beautiful.

Protect her truest, most enduring beauty, boys. Protect what's inside. Hide her eyes and her heart from the ridiculous standards and impossible expectations that our society has created. Tell her not to believe the lies of the media. Those shows, those magazines, those opinion leaders...they get paid to make her feel bad about herself. They'll tell her that her eyes are too small, or her clothes are out of style. Her eyelashes are too short, and her hair is too long. They'll tell her that her abs aren't flat enough and that her legs are too short. Protect her from those lies. She is, as God intended, perfect.

Oh yeah, one more thing, boys. Remember that we age too. We'll get older, and slower, and less muscular, and probably bald! So, keep that in mind. :)

That inner beauty, though; that beauty that took you beyond physical attraction and made you fall in love; that beauty that made your heart ache when you were apart…that kind of beauty never goes away. Like a rose bush: the more you tend to it, the more beautifully it grows.

Boys, I want you to appreciate the only timeless beauty that ever exists…and that beauty is deeper than the skin.

Look for it.

See it.

Appreciate it.

…and tell her she's beautiful.

I love you,

Dad

15

Five Words

I was 40 when my first son arrived. That was no coincidence. Had I started my family any earlier, I am certain that my boys would not be growing into the young gentlemen that they are today. Tonight, 13-odd years later, is a night that I will fondly remember forever.

Tonight, I walked into the house from the garage to the sound of laughter in the kitchen. What better sound to walk in to? Michael had his shirt pulled up over his belly and he said, "Look, Jeffrey! I don't have a six-pack. I've got a one-pack." Although he was laughing, and although he's a great-lookin' kid, he has always been self-conscious about his belly being "too big."

Truth be told, his tummy has stuck out a bit since he was a baby. I remember taking pictures of him when he was just a toddler, then sending them off to his doctor, wondering if there was some sort of GI issue. At its worst, as early as two years old, he looked nine months pregnant, then within an hour or so, he looked quite typical again.

Well, long story longer, Michael's self-imposed 'New Year's resolution' was to become a fitter, strong, healthier kid. "Maybe we could go to the gym together, Dad. Not every day, but maybe two or three days a week?" This sounded like a great idea. His resolution. His terms.

Back to the laughter.

After looking at Michael, laughing with his shirt pulled up, and hearing his brother and him laughing uncontrollably, I started laughing myself. But, as soon as I started laughing, I had this horrible thought that he would think I might be laughing *at* him as opposed to *with* them. It was time to—immediately but subtly—remind him that I loved him, absolutely and unconditionally.

At that point in time, injuries had kept me from my normal exercise routine, so I was 15 pounds heavier than I wanted to be…and I was feeling it! I quickly looked at Michael's belly, then into his eyes, then paused for a moment. I was thinking, *I know in my heart that he loves me, respects me, and admires me. I know that he watches me put in endless hours of training. I know that he has had tears in his eyes when he's seen me cross the finish-line on race days.* So, with a grin on my face, I pulled my shirt up, stuck out my belly a bit and said, "See, buddy? I've got a one-pack too! We can work on 'em together, OK?"

That's when he said it! That's when he blew my mind. He looked up from what he was doing, for just a split second, and said, "Five words, Dad! Five words."

The feeling that came over me was unlike anything I'd ever felt. It was a combination of humility, gratitude, pride, love, and disbelief, all turned up to 11!

That phrase, "Five words," evolved over the thousands of hours spent tucking him in at night. Some tuck-ins were long and filled with growing pains; some were short, peaceful, and full of love. With the passing months and years, "I love you" became "I love you, buddy." Then it was

"I love you to the moon." As he grew into his middle-school years it became crucial that he knew, in his most challenging moments, that no matter what…I loved him exactly as he was.

So, what are those five words?

"Just the way you are."

That night, I showed him that I'm self-conscious too, and that I've got weaknesses and doubts, and perceived imperfections too. When I shared my fears and insecurities with him, his immediate, almost unconscious response was just that…

"Five words, Dad. Five words."

All of those hours by his side, for all of those years and all of those tears, not only gave him the love he needed but gave him enough to pass it along. I never dreamed that, very directly, I would become the recipient of the love that I had given. I had literally reaped what I'd sown.

"And in the end, the love you take is equal to the love you make." ~ The Beatles

If you have kids, or when you have kids, remember this: We are not here to praise them for doing what they're told, to love them for doing what we think is right. We are here to love our children, period. Unconditional love is the single greatest, most inspiring, most transformative, most nurturing act we could ever do for our kids—or for anyone, for that matter. The absence of love is the single most devastating and destructive force I've ever seen. So, love 'em with all of their imperfections. In fact, love them because of those imperfections. When they make mistakes (and they will), guide them, direct them, set expectations for them, challenge them, and love them just the way they are.

Mikey…you're a special boy with a compassionate and loving heart. I love you, son…five words.

16

Self-Esteem Comes from Ourselves

"Self-esteem is the reputation we acquire with ourselves."
– NATHANIEL BRANDEN

Hey guys! It's Dad.

First, I love you. You're wonderfully, beautifully, perfectly human. Five Words. Right?

Just the way you are!

So, what is self-esteem? Self-esteem is how we see ourselves and how we value ourselves. It's based on our opinions and beliefs about our perceived strengths and weaknesses, which can feel difficult to change. Self-esteem affects our self-confidence. Our self-esteem can affect whether we appreciate ourselves or disrespect and dishonor ourselves.

It took me a long time to actually understand self-esteem (or lack thereof) before I could start to use that awareness and understanding as a tool. Now I use those thoughts, emotions, fears, and insecurities like a sort of barometer as to how I'm doing in my life as a whole. When I'm feeling down or disappointed about myself, my performance, or my behavior I ask questions such as: Would I be my friend? Would I hire myself? Would I trust myself? Do I even like myself? Do I have a level of self-esteem (enough value) that will give me the confidence to stand up for myself? Do I subordinate my values, feelings, thoughts, ideas, and needs in order to make others feel better or to fit in? Can I stand on my own? If the answer to those questions is yes, I look at why I think that way. If the answer is no...I ask, "Why not?" which helps me dive into what I need to do to fix it!

Psychologists are constantly adding to an already bloated list of causes for low self-esteem or feelings of inadequacy. These causes include: Lower than normal physical or academic performance, disapproval from authority or parents, social beauty standards, emotionally disengaged or neglectful parents, and many others.

But let's look at this from a new perspective, a difference that I don't see as semantic. "Esteem" literally means to respect and admire, and we all know what "Self" means. But if self-esteem means the presence or absence of respect and admiration toward ourselves...how can we hold others accountable for the state of the way we view ourselves? Shouldn't self-esteem—or, for that matter, a lack of self-esteem—be attributed to us...not them?

I heard author Jay Shetty once say, "Whatever you want from someone else, give it to yourself first! If you want compliments from someone else, give them to yourself first. If you want validation or praise from someone else, give it to yourself first." If we can't give ourselves those compliments...what do we need to do, what actions do we need to take in order to believe that we deserve them? How can we expect more from others than we're willing to do ourselves?

As a teacher, I've had many tear-filled conversations with high school students who finally recognize how poorly they view themselves. It typically goes something like this...

Me: "If I told you a secret, would you keep it? If your brother or your boyfriend told you a secret, would you keep it?"

Student: "Yes. I can't imagine sharing someone else's private things with someone else. We don't even have a right to do that."

Me: "Why not? OK, but what if they didn't tell you to promise not to tell anyone?"

Student: "I still wouldn't tell. That would break their trust in me. It would be mean. I just couldn't do that. I would hope that they wouldn't tell my secrets if I shared one with them."

Me: "You're showing respect and compassion and understanding toward your friend."

Student: "Yeah! It's easy when you care about them!"

Me: "But earlier this week you told me that you were gonna get more sleep, eat better, and not allow yourself to be distracted so you could get caught up on your schoolwork. You made that commitment to yourself. You know how important it is, not just to you but to your family, that you graduate on time. You deserve that. Did you keep that promise to yourself?"

Student: "No."

Me: "Why not?"

Student: "I don't know."

Me: "Why did you keep that commitment to your friend?"

Student: "Because I care about her. I respect her and her feelings, and just being a decent human being!"

Me: "So you don't care about you? You don't respect you and your feelings? You don't think you deserve the same love and care and respect as your friend."

That brief conversation is usually followed by silence, awareness, acceptance, then tears.

We all do it. Well, most of us, anyway. We make commitments to others—our bosses, our spouses, our kids, our neighbors or extended family members. We keep 'em all. But when it comes to promises to ourselves—"I'm gonna go back to the gym five days a week!" "I'm gonna spend less time on social media." "I'm gonna quit drinking soda." "I'm gonna put my phone down thirty minutes before I go to sleep."—we almost immediately break those commitments. The fact that we don't respect ourselves as much as a colleague or neighbor is sad and far too common.

Maybe our self-esteem really is "from us." Maybe we shouldn't be looking for praise and acceptance and acknowledgement from others until we're willing to give ourselves the very same thing. Maybe we can notice when we're undermining our own views of ourselves and use those as triggers to challenge those beliefs. Find examples of skills or talents or character traits that you do possess. Think of something you contribute to. Think of something kind or supportive you've done for someone else...even if they never noticed or never thanked you! Maybe all you did was listen. But that in itself has become a lost art! Listening! And you did that! Big or small. Noticed or not! You still did something kind for someone else.

Clearly the girl in the conversation above lacked true self-respect—but she was honest, trustworthy, and integral in her friend's life, and what character traits are more important than those?

What do you do if you truly can't think of a talent or skill or character trait or something kind that you did in the service of others? Then you have a blank slate! You have every opportunity to let this awareness trigger that change in you. The world is your oyster! Challenge yourself! Explore! Try things. Fail. Build a healthy, balanced relationship. Say no to people and things that aren't congruent with you, your values, and where you want to be.

Give, and find out how giving you are.

Live a little, and find out what life is about.

Laugh, and feel the happiness your laughter brings.

Love, and feel how loving you are.

I love you guys. I hope you love yourselves too.

Love, Dad.

17

My Stress, Anxiety, and Depression Toolbox

When it comes to the stresses of our lives, maybe Lennon & Mc-Cartney had the answer right from the start. We need to just "Let it be."

It's likely, however, that even those famous lyrics were inspired by wisdom passed down by the sages and mentors who guided Liverpool's famous composing duo.

Reading and listening to books from the most recognized social and spiritual leaders is where I've found the ideas that guide me through life's challenges. Some of these books are thousands of years old, and some are brand new, but the lessons and points of view that they all contain are timeless. Through these lessons and through new eyes, I see stress, worries, and depression very differently than I did when I suffered more acutely in the past. Implementing and practicing these lessons helps me find peace, even in my darkest and most worrisome times.

At the time I initially started this post, my boys and I were nearing the end of our summer break. As two teens and a middle school teacher, we were each facing new school years, a change of schools, meeting new people, and as always…we were poised to write the next chapters in our lives. It's times like these when we can find ourselves bound by the chains of worry and the fears of what lies ahead. What better time to share what I've learned over the years about all sorts of uncomfortable, awkward, and often unhealthy feelings that we're certain to all experience at one time or another?

I wish that I had handled fear and stress differently when I young. I wish that I could say that these worries, these anxiety-filled moments will end as we move through life, but they won't. They only change. They turn from worries about fitting in to worries and fears about careers and friendships and starting a family and health concerns and on and on. The sooner we learn to see stress for what it actually is, the better off we'll be moving forward toward bigger and better and most importantly… happier times.

Of the thousands of pages that I've read on the subject, here is a simplification of the thoughts and ideas of our wisest and most informed, as they pertain to stress, anxiety, and depression:

All stress is caused by our inability or unwillingness to accept what is. Read that again.

All stress is caused by our inability or unwillingness to accept what is.

It creeps or sometimes bursts into our lives during the times when we either can't accept or refuse to accept our current life circumstances. Accepting what is…is the simplest key to calm feelings of stress, anxiety, shame, regret, anger, disappointment, sadness, and so on.

Before we go too much further, it's important to know that there are actually two very different types of emotional stress: Eustress and Distress. Eustress, like euphoria, is fantastic; it's positive! Distress breaks us down, and when left unattended…it can bring us to our knees.

Eustress has the following characteristics: It motivates us, and it focuses our energy and intentions. It is short-term, and it's something within our realm of control. Although it's still a type of stress and it feels uncomfortable—it can bring tears and even make you feel nauseous—it's really an exciting feeling. And when we can harness its power to actually improve our mental and physical performance, it's one of life's most beautiful tools. You might be coming out of a coach's huddle, heading onto the basketball court with 3.8 seconds left and the championship on the line, or you may be waiting for the curtain to open on the biggest stage you've ever performed on. Either way...your chemistry changes. You can feel the energy running through your veins. It's almost electric!

Distress, however, is bad. It's very bad. It's insidious. Distress, what we usually simply call "stress," is a negative stress that has the following characteristics: Distress makes us worry, it causes anxiety, and maybe worst of all it robs you of the moment that you're in! It robs you of focus and guides you away from your purpose and your intentions. It causes a release of chemicals in your body that literally makes you sick and miserable. It causes headaches. It steals your ability to focus and replaces it with fear and worry and so many other negative thoughts and feelings.

Today, stress accompanies us almost everywhere—our jobs, our homes, our meals, and our bedrooms. We don't even need to give it an invitation. It first sneaks into our minds, then slowly finds its way into our spirits, eating away at our passions like a cancer. It will suck enthusiasm and life and love from even simplest joys. Distress is all-consuming and doesn't discriminate...it can get to you even in the best of times. Distress can be long-term or short-term, but it's often perceived as outside of our ability to control. The accompanying feelings are not exciting. In fact, they're quite unpleasant. Stress has been repeatedly, scientifically proven to decrease both mental and physical performance.

But how bad can it really be? I mean…c'mon! Harden up!

When left unchecked, stress literally becomes a silent assassin. I don't share that lightly…because it hits so close to home. Research shows that our inability to manage stress levels leads to heart disease, asthma, obesity, headaches, intestinal problems, premature death, and depression. Even more tragic, like voodoo and black magic, it can draw us in, enticing the most vulnerable to search for permanent solutions to life's temporary problems.

Recognizing the unique natures of these two different stresses, we can see that eustress is absolutely fantastic. It's often the antidote we need in order to break free. But now let's focus on distress—learning how to recognize it, how to avoid it, and how to untangle it when we need to.

Perhaps the most important revelation that I've come across when searching for remedies for anxiety, stress, and depression is this:

There are only two primary, fundamental causes for our emotional distress, but they are both solved by the same solution. Two problems. One solution. This means that if we can (and yes, some will certainly require more clinical/medical remedies) master just one solution…we can use that to help us through all of our challenging emotional times. So, what is that elusive, mysterious solution?

Simply and directly, we need to be present. We need to learn to "Be in the now." We have to accept our life circumstances…as they are right now. Make peace with it. Become its partner. "Now" is the only moment we've ever had…and the only moment we will ever have.

But how does it work? Adopting this mentality may not be easy, as we've had years and years of practice worrying, and little to no time learning and practicing mindfulness.

It works like this:

All feelings of guilt, shame, anger, resentment, bitterness, and sadness result from living in the past. "How could I be so stupid?" "I can't believe he could betray me like that!" "Why did this have to happen to me?" "It's not fair that this happened in the first place!" "I just can't forgive her." Can't you feel the pain written into all of those comments? All of these comments, every last one, focus on something behind us; something that happened in our past, not in our present moment. In fact, in a very real, very literal, very scientific way…those events are no longer real. We can't find them. We can't measure them. We can't record them. They are gone, unless or until we invite them back into our lives. If we're present, we can see; we can feel…that they aren't actually with us.

Next…

All feelings of anxiety, fear, worry, insecurity, and that general uneasiness that's become so prevalent in modern societies…come from living in the future. Our worries about the future steal us from the moment we're in and bury us in fear about what may (or may not) come later. If we're not mindful and present we can find ourselves being hit by an avalanche of "What Ifs." "What if I don't get the job?" "What if she doesn't like me?" "What if the doctor can't help us?" "What if I'm not chosen?" Worrying about the future, regardless of what we're fearing or anxious about, will never improve our future. It will, with absolute scientific certainty, make it worse. But it will never make it better. Truth be told, we're often worrying about circumstances that we believe are coming, when in fact, they aren't! What a massive and undermining disservice this is to our wellness and our happiness. We rob ourselves of the "Now" by worrying about an event that will likely never happen in the future.

Personally, I often catch my mind wandering aimlessly through a sea of "What Ifs" only to remind myself that I am absolutely fine at the moment. I'm sitting on a comfortable sofa, in a beautiful home, with a cup of tea in my lap, surrounded by my boys. Really! What else could I possibly want? Why would I ever allow stress to rob that precious moment from me? I recognize stress and worry as an intruder…then I politely excuse it.

"But I've lost my job and…"

"But if he leaves me, I'll…"

Yes! There are so many "What Ifs" to worry about. But if you lost your job…do you want to be unemployed and miserable, or unemployed and grateful? In both cases you're unemployed. Worrying about it won't change that fact. Action will! Positivity will! So, what a perfect time to look at what we SHOULD do as opposed to what we shouldn't be doing.

The Best "Toolbox" I've Ever Built

Now that we've taken a moment to recognize the ugly truth about allowing stress, anxiety, and depression to take us away from our present moments, how do we fix it?

It's important that I take a second to state something clearly: Anxiety and depression are dreadful mental and emotional foes. Periodically, individuals do and should lean on modern medicines for relief. I'm certainly not a doctor. I'm not even an expert. In fact, I've had a lot of failures in this area over the decades. In fact, I've gotten incredibly good at failing. So much so that it doesn't feel any different to me than making my bed in the morning or taking out the trash. Failure is a function of success, and man…it is a wise and powerful teacher. Finding solutions that don't work has helped me discover and hold on to some tools that are actually effective (for me) in pushing back the dark!

I now keep a funny little visual in my head of a small toolbox; one like my dad used to call our family's "crash kit." Not over-dramatizing for effect, but this little "toolbox" has literally saved my life on more than a few occasions. It's a sort of laundry list of strategies that we can always use to help manage sad, lonely, and hurtful feelings when they start to show their ugly faces. We can learn to recognize them earlier and earlier, then stop them in their tracks and escort them to the exit.

Stay grounded in gratitude.

Focus on what you have now…in this moment. Is it family? Maybe a close friend? Your relationship with God? A place to sleep? A meal? Focus on your safety, your health, or anything else that's going right, rather than what you perceive is going wrong. I've had instances in my life where things were incredibly difficult to get through, but simply being grateful for the bed I slept in and the fact that I could see and hear helped me get through those moments. A bed. Sight. The ability to hear. That's literally all I could find. Maybe that's not all that I had to be grateful for, but it's all I could find in the moment…and it was enough, enough to help me through the next moment. Gratitude and anxiety live in the same place in your head. Focusing on gratitude gives anxiety its eviction papers!

Think "Water."

If you find yourself feeling down, angry, on the verge of tears (not that tears are inherently bad), try to get closer to water. This probably seem ambiguous—"get close to water." It is! But water soothes the soul. It really does. It's what we're made of. It is our life force. So, pick one of these…or better…pick 'em all!

Jump in the pool, the ocean, a creek, run through the sprinklers…or just take a cold shower (Yes, cold! Shockingly cold). An ice bath or cold shower shocks our bodies and reaches beyond what's in our minds into what's often referred to as our "reptilian brain." Think about animals in nature. They don't worry. We do. Our animal instinct won't let us worry, so engaging that part of our brain can help us focus on what matters. It helps us be present. How many times in the movies do you see someone panicking, only to have someone else throw a glass of water in their face? Add to that this scientific fact: Water in motion releases negative ions. Negative ions are odorless, tasteless molecules that we inhale while we're near them. Negative ions have been proven to reduce stress and help elevate our moods! So get to the pool, the river, the sea, and especially waterfalls. It works. It brings us to "the here and now."

Drink fresh, very cold water. Water, especially cold water, has a naturally calming effect. You can feel its effects, both physically and emotionally, almost the moment it hits your lips. There's a nice side effect to this strategy as well. While that tall glass or bottle of cold water is calming our mind and our emotions, our physical body is being hydrated and nourished, which is beneficial as well. Water is almost like a lubricant that helps our minds, bodies, and spirits function at their best.

Look within.

Don't look outside of yourself for solutions. Don't look to someone else to ease your pain. Caffeine, sugar, video games, adrenaline, shopping, relationships, etc. are never the answer. We may see our friends turning toward other vices such as drugs, alcohol, and prescription medications to help them "feel better." But there's one unequivocal truth about these "solutions": They all take more than they give. Sugar leaves us flat. Video games leave us tired and our brains fried. Comfort food makes us sleepy and causes unnecessary weight gain and a sea of other health issues. Depending on others to ease our discomfort may leave us lost if we find ourselves on our own again. Drugs, including alcohol and many prescription medications, may make you feel fantastic at the moment but often leave you feeling dreadful when they wear off. Again…they take more than they give.

Sit with your discomfort.

Here's the part where Lennon & McCartney (and Leo Babauta, from whom I first learned this technique) got it right. "Let it be." Let our stress, anxiety, fear, regret, or disappointment simply be. We can sit with our pain. See it. Feel it. Notice it. Watch it change. If we sincerely give it our attention…it will change. It always changes. In a way, it's a healthy means of processing our stress. When we're done, it's gone…or at least much more manageable. Yes, it may come back. But recognizing the emotion for what it is, then watching it change into something completely different can be a lifesaving skill.

Get physical.

This one is very special to me. Depending on the severity of your negative emotion in the moment—depending on your immediate level of discomfort—you may want to get really physical! Intensely physical! There's a phrase that I lean on from time to time that reads, "Mood follows action." I think of this almost like bump-starting a car with a dead battery. The car won't run. It won't start. So, let's push it or roll it down a hill (action)…then pop the clutch and let it run (mood).

Sometimes simply taking a walk can help get us re-centered. For me though, it often takes something a bit more intense to steal my thoughts back from my fears and anxieties, so I go to a level of intensity that works. With practice, you'll learn to recognize the feelings almost like a headache. You'll feel them getting better. It might take a trip to the gym or a quick bike ride or a run. But during those instances when I can't get away (restless at 2:30am, at work, etc.) I can still knock out a few sets of pushups or sit-ups, just enough to get my mind off of what's consuming my thoughts at that moment. Make it intense. You'll have to focus on what you're doing in the moment which leaves no mind left to perpetuate your suffering.

Feed your body.

I don't mean sit on the sofa with a Little Caesar's pizza and a Coke. For real. That's not even food. I mean feed yourself. Take in the fuel that our minds, bodies, and spirits need. Don't feed the emotion what emotion needs. Feed your body what your body needs! For me, it's all about fresh whole foods. It might be a fruit salad or green salad. More often, it's a smoothie that's packed with everything our bodies could possibly need. I'm not a doctor or a nutritionist, so I can't be sure what I'm lacking. So, during really challenging emotional times I 'top it all off.' What I call my "Fix-All" smoothie starts with coconut water, turmeric powder, and flax meal or chia seeds. I add to that nutrient- and vitamin-rich spinach or kale (that I've cleaned, blanched, and frozen in advance). Take a base like that, then add your favorite fruit (or whatever's on the counter about to go bad). Typically, I keep frozen blueberries, strawberries, raspberries, mango, and pineapple in the freezer. In a very real way, my freezer is my medicine cabinet. I keep it stocked with all I need, from ice packs to organic fruits and veg. "Let food be thy medicine and medicine be thy food." I think that Hippocrates guy could be onto something.

Breathe with purpose.

Breathing with intention is an incredibly powerful way to bring yourself and your thoughts together again. Think about that. It's a powerful way to bring yourself…and your thoughts…together.

This is a skill that the East has mastered, and the West won't even give credence to. Often, taking a short moment to focus on a few (7 to 10) full breaths is enough to get your body and mind back in line. Don't think about posture. In fact, let that go. We want to breathe! Big, full, belly-stretching breaths. As you continue to practice breathing, those 7 to 10 breaths will turn into 3 to 5...then it will become one. Now... it takes me one, big, deep, focused, intent-filled breath in order to let the stresses of the moment fall away. In fact, the power of breath is so evident in science that there are a number of experts who believe that the "Runner's High"—that feeling we sometimes feel during and after a great run—is more about the heavy breathing than it is about the actual running itself. Whatever activity that requires heavy breathing would probably do just fine! Get creative...

Do something.

Well, isn't that ambiguous? Yeah. It's designed that way. It leaves the door open to interpretation, circumstance, and ability. It takes away excuses. So... do something. Find anything to do; anything that requires your attention. Do something good for yourself, like yoga or reading. Do a chore, but do it with focus and attention. Do schoolwork. Do something for someone else. As a busy dad, this can be something as simple as making sure that the kitchen is clean or folding the laundry. But, while I'm folding towels and socks and pajamas, my focus is on the task. Other than maybe some soft sounds or music in the background, I make sure that my environment is peaceful. Then...I focus on the task at hand and doing it absolutely perfectly. The folds are symmetric. The stacks are neat like you see at Macy's or Nordstrom. It focuses my attention on the task at hand...leaving no room for whatever else had previously captured my attention. Bonus? Now you're done with the laundry or the dishes or the vacuuming. The key is to just get engaged in something that requires your full attention to do it right. Can't think of anything? Write a thank you note. Really! Just take a moment to write a sincere, hand-written thank you note. It's sad that this simple, kind, and courteous gesture has all but vanished. "But I don't have stamps" (we can be awesome at making excuses). So write your thank you note, then take a picture of it and text it to the recipient. I promise…it will be appreciated.

This last tool, doing something, actually brings us right back to the beginning—right back to #1 again. In order to write a sincere thank you note, you need to be in a place of gratitude. That place of gratitude is where our journey out of the dark should always start.

And as for this incomplete laundry list of thoughts and ideas? You can do several of these at the same time, or even sequentially. Do what works for you, but I find that by the time I've done one or two of them, I've collected my thoughts and I've centered myself again, and often with a happier, more peaceful disposition. If one or two haven't worked, I continue down the list until I find relief.

At the end of the day, all we need to do is to engage in an activity that commands our attention and forces us to be present.

When we're living in the moment, fully accepting the moment that we're in, we'll no longer experience the regrets, sadness, or disappointments of the past, nor will we suffer through the anxieties, worries, or fears of our future.

Stay in the moment. Accept what is. The rest will take care of itself.

If you know someone who's struggling with anxiety and depression, please pass this list along. I can't promise that it will help, but it can't hurt.

I love you guys.

Dad

18

The Unseen Battles of Others

"Be kind; for everyone you meet is fighting a hard battle."

Although often misattributed to Plato, this quote originated from a Scottish writer named Ian Maclaren.

On the surface, this post might appear to be just another attempt to sprinkle a bit of sunshine on your day; but it truly isn't. It's a gentle reminder to redirect our emotions away from judgment and toward a happier, more fulfilling place.

I often hear people whining on social media, "Oh yeah, right! What is she complaining about? She's got it made! Try living my life for a day... or an hour," or, "You've got to be kidding. This guy's depressed? Are you kidding me? He screwed up! Just cop to it! Sitting all alone in his ocean-view, Malibu home! Give me a break. Cry me a river! I can't even pay my rent this month!"

This sort of judgment, misunderstanding, or shortsightedness can lead to some pretty uncomfortable feelings within us from time to time. This is where the idea of "Everyone you meet is fighting a battle" comes into play. Perspective—the way we see something—really does change the thing we're seeing.

When I was in junior college, I worked for a car dealer in San Francisco's East Bay. I would show up after class each day to empty the trash from the mechanics' stalls, empty oil drain cans, do the odd repair, grab customers' cars from the back lot, etc. It wasn't a glamourous job, but at the same time, it was perfect.

I remember arriving at work one day to find the owner's youngest daughter sitting at my desk. Let's call her Donna. She was a mess. She was clearly in the midst of a real crisis, sobbing uncontrollably. She was sort of bouncing back and forth between what appeared to be a sincerely painful emotional breakdown and a full-on adult temper tantrum. It was painful to watch.

All I wanted to do was hug her to help her get through whatever had completely derailed her day. Work, though, was hardly an appropriate place for a hug, nor an emotional meltdown. But her older brother (my boss at the time) was sitting at his desk next to her. I knew that she was being cared for, so I just gave her a gentle squeeze on her shoulders for reassurance, then headed into the garage.

The next day she told me what had happened. "Yesterday was my 18th birthday," she said. She told me that she really wanted a new convertible Toyota Celica for her birthday, but she also wanted that sporty new MR2. The emotional breakdown that she had struggled through the day before came from the simple fact that her dad wouldn't get her both. Yes. Both cars.

Let that sink in for a moment.

When she shared that with me, I literally didn't know how to respond. It was like I was stuck. It felt like somebody had pushed the pause button on my life but forgot to press it on everyone else's.

The year before, my parents had let me borrow $900 to help buy my first car, my 15-year-old Chevy. Part of the reason I was working at the car dealership was that I still needed to pay them back. But Donna was distraught, inconsolable, over the fact that she couldn't get two brand-new cars for her birthday. She was upset because she had to pick one. I couldn't even grasp the concept.

Then, out of the blue (to this day, I don't know where the thought came from), I got it...I understood. I understood why this "non-issue" could be seen as the most tragic and challenging experience in Donna's lifetime. But how? How could it possibly be?

Because...it was.

In sharp contrast, one of my junior college study partners named Kriztien had recently escaped communist Hungary by hanging on the axel of a moving railroad car. His brother tried as well, but he fell off and didn't survive.

Donna's ordeal was clearly far less traumatic. But was it to her?

At that time, I believe that Donna's dilemma the was the most painful thing she had ever gone through. "Daddy" had always given her anything and everything she wanted. She was his little girl! He adored her. But this time he didn't give her what she wanted. This time, Daddy said no, and he meant it.

Imagine what this must have felt like for her. Did she think her dad didn't love her as much anymore? Eighteen years of bliss...shattered with a two-letter word; no. Was she worried about what was coming next? Was her father going to encourage her to move out and get a job? She had always enjoyed the most comfortable life, and this was, emotionally, the most uncomfortable and frightening thing that she'd ever experienced.

Kriztien risked getting run over by a train—only to be caught, arrested, imprisoned, then escaped from prison—then tried again to hang onto the axel of the exact same train a second time. All of this, simply to gain freedom. This was clearly the most terrifying experience of his life. I couldn't begin to imagine what that was like. When he got out of Hungary, he knew that he needed to get to Vienna to ensure his safety...and he did. But once in Vienna, he had absolutely no idea what life would be like over the next hour, much less over the next few years.

Donna's experience, although dramatically different on the surface, might have felt very much the same to her. She had no idea what was next, what caused her dad to change his behavior toward her, what her life would be like on the other side of this experience. She couldn't possibly know, and she was horrified.

Consider racing Usain Bolt, an Olympic Gold Medalist sprinter, for 100 meters. We can all run, but we often forget that sprinting as fast as we can for 100 meters is just as difficult for us as it is for Usain Bolt. In fact, it may be more difficult because we've never had to do it before. Donna had never had to do it before, while Kriztien had.

We all have our own battles that we're fighting, and very often those battles are challenges that we couldn't possibly have imagined. We don't have to judge them or compare them, to our own challenges or to anybody else's. Whether it's unhealthy coping strategies, physical or sexual abuse, money issues, worries about health problems, and/or family and relationship breakdowns, we're all going through something tough. We're all fighting through things that we don't really want to be fighting through. The most empathetic and compassionate thing we can do to help each other...to help ourselves...is simply to be kind. Be loving... toward everyone, everywhere you go, virtually or face to face.

Remember, too, that kindness is not an omission of malice but an action. Like love, "being kind" is an action. It is what we do.

Be sensitive of the battles that others are fighting. OK, guys? Then let your kindness shine through.

I love you guys.

Five Words.

Love, Dad

19

An Uncommon Cure to a Common Disease

"**D**isease" is an interesting term. Broken down, the word is more accurately understood: Dis-ease, or going against ease. It doesn't mean "sick." It can simply mean that you're not feeling peaceful or at ease.

Weather it's work, a seemingly endless global pandemic, exhaustion, a civil rights revolution, our president, how stupid the New York Nets are for trading away James Harden (OK...they're not) or why Starbucks can't seem to get my order right, we often carrying around feelings of, "Oh my gosh, I need to vent!" It feels good to unpack our day. It's nice to have someone to talk to, even if it's just to share our aggravations. But pay close attention to that feeling. It's less likely that we need to vent, and more likely that we need the exact opposite.

Anger, frustration, disappointment—these all-too-familiar feelings are not unique to any of us. The complications of living in a Westernized society often leave us feeling like we're being squeezed under the pressure of a sea of wrong-doers, wrong-doings, and an increased awareness that we are not living in alignment with our own individual values…but we can't seem to change course.

Often unconsciously, but sometimes consciously, we'll look for someone to share our aggravations with. We need to vent to someone, blow off some steam. Usually, it's our closest friends and families who are willing to sit with us and listen while we share what's eating at us. If they're not available, we'll bite our tongues for a bit, but ultimately, we'll take just about any unwitting victim who will lend an ear. It might be a colleague, an acquaintance, or the poor gal behind you in line at the supermarket.

But think about this short phrase from the paragraph above:

"…we'll look for someone to share our aggravations with. Usually, it's our closest friends and families…"

It's not like we're sharing a warm piece of apple pie or a bag of chips. We're sharing our pain. We're handing our pain, our disappointment, our aggravation, and our anger to those we love the most.

I want to make it clear that I understand the importance of community, family, friendships, and how the support and care of those around us lift us up, as we do in return, but consider this: After our sister, spouse, father, friend or colleague listens to our problems, we may catch ourselves saying something like, "Oh my gosh, I feel so much better now. Lighter. Thank you so much for listening." We might as well say, "Thanks for carrying all of my drama for me. It was getting unbearable. Clearly, you don't have anything in your own life to worry about, so thanks again for helping me carry mine!" And for the caring but unwitting victim, what's the reward? Probably another heavy, burden-dumping session next Monday at 4:30 'cuz, "I love you so much. You're always there for me."

Although it's a shame, it's no secret that we tend to dump our feelings onto those we're closest to. They care. It's that simple. But it's tragic, really. Let's sprinkle a dash of insult onto their new burden. We've just shined a modest light onto the human propensity to share with our loved ones the countless wrongdoings woven through our lives. So, what if I now tell you that most of those wrongdoings we've actually done to ourselves?

Although we may think that we are feeling angry or mistreated, these feelings are often just masks being worn by a different sort of internal conflict and frustration. It's not uncommon for our own underlying feelings of guilt, remorse, betrayal, or simply living out of alignment with our values to create inner conflict. "Why can't I seem to lose weight?" "I'm so tired of filling out applications and going to job interviews!" "If I had just gone to college right out of high school, I wouldn't be in this mess!" Then, when we're really digging into our own shortcomings, our barista shares with us that she's out of our favorite blend of coffee. Enter the creeper—that ego-driven voice that wants to be heard and justified and validated—which hijacks our consciousness and whispers, "Who can I talk to? Who can I complain to, so I feel better? Oh, I'm gonna see Carol at the gym. I can vent to her about how crummy this Starbucks always is! She's such a good listener."

What our egos are masking is the messages that we're actually saying to ourselves.

"I need Carol to validate my feelings. I need her to agree with me, so I know that I'm right and so that my feelings are justified. Good! Now I don't have to take responsibility for my feelings and my current life circumstance. Now, I don't have to work on myself. I can just point my finger at my spouse or my teachers or my barista."

What we're looking for when we vent is sympathy, or, better yet (and more contagious), empathy. Our ego needs to know that it's been wronged. And what's better than an ego that needs to vent? TWO egos, or maybe ten, or a thousand. Look at the mob mentalities ripping our country to shreds right now. While we're sinking, both socially and economically, our egos are absolutely THRIVING! Want to add even more fuel to the fire? Take our collective egos and tie them to a purpose! Now THAT is power! Give that purpose a name? Even better.

The truth is that we're behaving in ways that, to an outsider, look very much like we actually prefer conflict to peace. How we use our emotions is up to us, but only if we recognize that we are the ones in control.

Take atomic energy, for example. Nuclear power plants produce incredibly clean, cheap, and reliable energy, second only to wind in terms of cost per kilowatt-hour. But atomic energy also killed a quarter of a million people in the blink of an eye, during World War II. Our emotions and energy can be just as volatile and just as fickle. We can use our emotions and our energy to foster conflict or to foster peace. It's up to us.

So how do we catch ourselves? How do we stop ourselves from spewing forth our aggravations and negative energy onto our loved ones? How do we flip the script and share compassion and interest and care instead of pain?

All we have to do is recognize it.

Recognize it for what it is. Be aware. When you find yourself venting, or just as often piling your drama onto someone else who started the venting session, let that ugly feeling throw a penalty flag for you! *"Wait…I'm doing it again! I'm complaining again!"* Then…pause. Take a breath. Own it.

Then, next time you feel like, *"I can't wait to call my brother and tell him everything"* or *"I can't wait to tell my wife about this when I get home."* you need to do just that. You need to wait. Take a breath. Call your brother. But rather than complaining to him about the atrocities of your suburban day, ask him how he's doing. Ask him what makes him smile. Walk into your house and ask your spouse how his or her day was. Better than that, run into the house...with a flower (yeah, guys appreciate thoughtfulness too) and give your spouse a hug. Tell him or her that you're happy to be home, that you are grateful that you've got the job that you've got, then ask...lovingly and sincerely..."How was your day... and how is your heart?"

OK, they might look at you like you're crazy at first, but they'll get used to it. And imagine, what if that became normal? What if, rather than adding fuel to the fire everywhere we went, we brought cool, clean water to the fire? What if we listened more than we spoke? What if we thought about them more than we thought about ourselves? Remember, these are the ones we love more than any other. Right?

The amazing thing about our egos and their insatiable appetites for feeling important is that we don't have to kill them or force them to go away. If we just focus on others, if we listen, our egos simply dissolve and blow away—and with them...all the unnecessary weight that we've carried around in order to keep them fed.

So next time you're feeling like you need to call a buddy and say, "Man! Can I just vent for a second?" see that feeling for what it is, then pause. Smile. Make the call, then share that smile. Ask them how they're doing. "So, what keeps you smiling?" They're either going to give you the answer...or their ego is going to reach out and share all of their struggles with you. Wouldn't you rather be there for them than the other way around? If that's the case, be their sounding board. Be there for them. Listen. Hear the sound without echoing it back.

There's something extremely rewarding about entering a conversation with someone who's angry or hurt, then leaving them with a feeling of gratitude and a new, healthier, happier point of view. And when the conversation is over, you'll see that you've fed two birds with one hand (no need to kill the birds with a stone, right?). You'll notice that you're no longer feeling anger, frustration, and disappointment, and you'll notice that they're no longer hurting either. You told your ego to shut up and listen for a second, and you've practiced recognizing that your happiness is up to YOU, and you've stopped focusing on the fact that McDonald's screwed up your breakfast…again.

The more you practice this, the more rewarding it gets. Soon, you'll find yourself surrounded by people that appreciate you for the energy and light that you bring with you wherever you go.

I promise…it works.

I love you guys.

Five Words

Love, Dad

20

The Pause that Prevents Sorrow

Creating Space between Stimulus and Response

This post was written during a COVID lockdown of 2020. Regardless of the situation today, the thoughts, ideas, and strategies still hold true.

Being isolated right now is weighing on us all. Our routines flew out the window. Our anxieties are through the roof. Tempers are frayed. Our futures unknown. It's not an easy time for any of us. Pausing to remember that, for others as much as for ourselves, is an important tool to master.

Like many in the developed world, my schedule, albeit self-imposed, is pretty ridiculous. I won't bore you with the logistics of teaching, coaching, training, writing, and being a single dad of two high-school boys. But I will share the importance of occasionally clocking out to ground myself. The frequency and duration of these little breaks vary depending on circumstances, but they're necessary for the purging of mental and physical stress.

When I allow myself, remind myself, or force myself to unplug for a moment, no matter how brief, it's always rejuvenating. It helps me refuel emotionally. It's like a reset button. As a result, I tend to become a gentler, kinder human being. It fosters humility, so I become a humbler person; a more grounded brother and son; a more inspired teacher and friend; and most importantly, a more patient, understanding, and loving father. What's that worth? It's priceless.

That said, something happened while I was on a hot and hilly trail run the other day. An uncommon occurrence literally stopped me in my tracks. But before I prematurely pulled the plug on my run and dug in for what was bound to be an unpleasant experience, I became very aware of the tension that resides somewhere between reaction and response. I recognized just how difficult it can be to master the latter and not succumb to the prior.

Nineteen minutes into what really needed to be a solid, uncomfortable, and ego-stripping run, I received a text from one of my boys:

"Dad, I'm sorry to interrupt your run, but Jeffrey is being so annoying right now! I don't know why, but he won't stop. He does this whenever you leave the house now. Will you please call him or text him and tell him to stop? Please?" (Truth: This never happens. Ever. Michael and Jeffrey are absolutely best friends. They're as respectful of each other as they are of their friends, family, and teachers.)

I was just getting into the steep and twisty single-track trails when the text came through. I was doing my best to, with an intentional spirit of proactively, digest and contemplate the concerns of our times, to talk to God, to appreciate the sun and the fresh air after being locked down for what seemed like forever. Then the message came.

I almost came unglued (also something that never happens).

I clenched my jaw, closed my eyes in disbelief, and shook my head. Clenching my fists, my eyes darted back and forth, from the sky to the trail to the message on my phone, and back again. I didn't know where this was going to lead, but it wasn't going to be pleasant!

"Siri! Call home!" I said with a jaw so angrily clenched that I wasn't sure that Siri would even recognize my voice.

I thought, or rather, the thought arose, *"If I can't step away for 20 (expletive deleted) minutes without you two…blah blah blah blah blah… then things are gonna change, boys! I don't know how much more you want from me…blah blah blah…"*

My mind ran through every iteration of cliched-parent-response ever uttered!

Alone, on the trail, I was actually embarrassed of my own thoughts, thinking, *"This just isn't like me!"* Then, as quickly as I called and just before the phone rang…I hung up.

I paused.

I closed my eyes.

I took a breath.

Here's the space. The space in time that will determine the future. I had been here before. I had practiced this moment. I knew better than to react. Never, ever react.

I flashed back to a moment when my boys were little. It wasn't an easy time. In this particular moment, my wife was in a hospital bed in our living room. I was in a sling after a shoulder surgery. I had just, literally single-handedly, cooked dinner and cleaned up. Now it was time for baths and pajamas. Pajamas? Oh yeah. They were in the dryer. So I grabbed a load of laundry and dumped it on the bathroom counter so I could watch my little one in the bath while I did my best to fold towels, socks, pajamas, and sheets with one arm.

It was a challenge. Aggravating, to say the least. Then, from the bathtub, "Hi Dadda!" "Hey handsome!" I responded, thinking less about the loving "Hi Dadda" and more about *How can I fold this without it sliding off the counter onto the bathroom floor?* There it was again, "Hi Dadda!" He was now looking at me through the reflection in the window above the tub. I looked over and smiled. "Hey buddy! I love you." Another couple pairs of socks tucked into each other, then... "Hi Dadda!" from the tub again. My temper was pretty shot. My spirt was pretty empty. I took a gentle pause and looked over at the cutest little kid ever, with a shampoo horn atop his head and water pouring...not from the faucet, but from my phone.

In that moment, something really rewarding happened. The "pause" to make space between stimulus and response, it just happened. I didn't have to try. I instinctively knew that there was no point in yelling; my phone was already beyond saving with a bag of rice. My gut reaction was to crouch down next to the tub and hold my hand to my ear and pretend that I was talking to him while he held my tragically dripping phone. "Hey, handsome boy! What did you do at work today?" He was loving me. He was showing me that he wanted to be like me. Like always, it was a time to love.

Yes. It was a hit on the budget. But...I snatched fear (my son fearing me) from the jaws of life. I'm sure that he doesn't remember this moment. That phone became the bath-time phone. He knew that my new phone didn't go in the bath...because then it wouldn't work anymore. I learned how good it feels to respond kindly as opposed to reacting unconsciously, harshly.

Back to the Trail

Like I said, I had been here before. I calmly and from a place of compassion thought, *"Wow. Poor kid. That's really out of character for him. They're awesome together. I wonder why he's behaving like this?"* Then came another quick pause. *"Ahhhhh. No, I don't. I don't wonder. I get it."*

I stepped ten or twelve inches off the trail and I squatted down. My eyes gazed down at the dirt and weeds below my feet, and my heart broke. I had a completely involuntary and powerful physical response to the emotions that had overcome me in that moment. My eyes welled up. The emotions became physically evident by the clear, visible trail the tears left as they cut through the dust that stuck to the sweat on my face. I lost my breath. I also lost my anger.

My heart broke because I could put myself in Jeffrey's shoes. I did my best to imagine what it must be like for a 12- or 14-year-old kid to go through what we're going through right now. He misses his girlfriend. He wants to have band practice. He misses the beach and our weekly "OK, you pick!" dinner outings. He wants to hoop it up with Michael and his high school buddies. They want to laugh; not maniacally as an uncontrolled protest of our current circumstances, but innocently. They miss their friends. They miss school. And in spite of the stoic faces that they don each morning…and their willingness to stand tall…they're scared. They are scared and confused.

After the Pause

I texted Michael back right away. *"I'm sorry, buddy. I'll be home in 10! OK?"* I didn't text Jeffrey. I let him sit for a moment to process his behavior on his own. I let him decide his own immediate and appropriate self-imposed "time out."

When I got home, I patted Michael on the head and told him that I loved him. Then I saw Jeffrey sitting on the couch with his phone. I sat down next to him and pulled him over against me. "How are you, buddy? I missed you on my run, so I thought I'd just come home early. I just wanted to be together right now. Is that cool?" He was so quiet. "Wanna watch Disney Plus or maybe some 2Hype on YouTube?" I asked. He accepted the hug and cuddled up to me like he was four years old again. He didn't cry, but he was hurting. I could feel it.

Jeffrey didn't deserve a reaction from me regardless of his behavior. He didn't deserve the "blah blah blah." He didn't deserve an ear full of misdirected anger and aggravation. He deserved a well-thought-out response. He deserved compassion. Don't we all? In turn, I didn't deserve to live with the guilt and sorrow of knowing that I'd thrown my personal baggage and pain onto my undeserving kids' shoulders.

So, yeah, I loved him. I loved him like he was four, because that was the proper response. Then, just like that, all was right. OK, all was not right in the world, but it was in my heart and in theirs.

This is a time for love...and for patience...and for compassion. It's a time for growth and a time for pause. It's time to practice our ability to interrupt our knee-jerk reactions, to create space between stimulus and response. It's time to pause and think with a compassionate heart, and then give our absolute best. It's time for us to love each other.

21

The Surfer's Mindset

Hey guys! It's Dad.

I've been throwing around this idea for quite some time—that surfing is a sort of metaphor for life. Not only that events in life come through in waves, but how we surf those waves ultimately determines our happiness.

It all kinda sorted itself out when I saw a social media post from a guy named David Bederman, called "The Surfers' Mentality."

To summarize, David explains that surfers do one particular thing better than most of us, and it's not surfing. Surfers want to catch a great wave! They'll fly and drive and hike and paddle and wait...to catch that perfect wave. But when they do, they know that it isn't going to last forever. When they drop in on a great wave, they really enjoy it, they ride it as long as they can. But at every moment, they know that the wave is gonna crash. They could wipe out. "Get drilled." But the surfer understands that there's always going to be another wave.

Wrapping this into thoughts of presence and gratitude, let me expand a little on his idea.

The way I see it is that surfers are better at being (and staying) present than most of us are. They don't take the good times, the bad times, or any of the times in between for granted.

When we go surfing, we need to be prepared. We need to be at the right place. If we're smart, if we've eaten, if we've stretched and warmed up a bit, thrown on some sunscreen, and waxed our boards...then we're prepared for the moments to come. We're hoping for good conditions; friends, both old and new; nice weather; and big, surfable waves. If all that lines up nicely for us, then we paddle out and wait.

Maybe we're stuck in the lull between sets. Maybe we miss the perfect wave as we're paddling out. But then we catch a good one. We're up... for a second, or five, or twenty. Maybe the nose of the board pearls. Maybe the wave closes out or we get sucked over the falls. Maybe we have a great, great ride and we let out a huge, hearty howl as we kick out, flopping on our back with our arms spread. But no matter what (unless maybe we got drilled) we'll just paddle out again, feel the sun on our faces, and smile.

The idea of not just being present, but also being grateful during good times and patient and understanding during challenging times, speaks to the impermanence of life. The presence and patience and appreciation and understanding—no matter what you are currently going through in life—ensures that you'll truly experience life with the best spirit possible. We can't be sure what's coming...but we can be sure that it's gonna be different. Ultimately, good or bad, every moment is temporary...unless we're unwilling see them that way.

But this "Surfer's Mentality" isn't actually a new thing. The same perspective—the same ideas of presence and gratitude and impermanence—can be found in old Jewish and Persian folklore dating back to 2,000 years before surfing was a thing. There are countless versions of fables, from King Solomon to Sufi poets to Abraham Lincoln, sharing one common idea: "This too shall pass."

Lincoln once spoke,

"It is said an Eastern monarch once charged his wise men to invent him a sentence, to be ever in view, and which should be true and appropriate in all times and situations. They presented him the words: 'And this, too, shall pass away.' How much it expresses! How chastening in the hour of pride! — how consoling in the depths of affliction!"

To be humbled by and grateful for the good times. To be understanding and graceful during the hard times...

To be present...

This is the surfer's mindset.

I love you guys.

Five Words

Love, Dad

22

Love Is a Verb

Hey guys! It's Dad!

I don't often quote the Bible, but this one sure fits the idea I wanted to share with you today.

"Dear children, let us not love with words or speech but with actions and in truth." ~John 3:18

"I love you."

When those words are sincere, heartfelt, there's almost no better feeling. But words aren't love. They may be beautiful, articulate, filled with rhetoric and art and expression and passion and truth. They may inspire deeds of love. They may be so persuasive and impactful that they change the course of dreams and lives and families and generations to come. But, in and of themselves they aren't love. Saying it doesn't make it so.

If you've ever felt love—true love—you know how magical it can feel. That emotion is the highest form of joy, at least as far as I've experienced. That emotion, that feeling…it's a thing. It's a noun. So how do we find that thing? How do we feel that thing? Perhaps most important, how do we keep that love alive?

I have felt what I thought was love. I have loved. I have felt true, effortless, inspiring, energizing, exciting, passionate love. And I have lost it. Many of us have. But through my desire to love I wanted to learn more about how to keep love thriving, vibrant, new, fresh…like a first kiss. Through my readings and watchings I came across the following conversation between author/mentor/coach Stephen Covey and a close friend of his who had fallen out of love with his wife. It changed how I see love, how I feel love, and how I give love…forever.

Mr. Covey's friend dejectedly shared, "My wife and I just don't have the same feelings for each other we used to have. I guess I just don't love her anymore and she doesn't love me. What can I do?"

"The feeling isn't there anymore?" Covey asked.

"That's right," he reaffirmed. "And we have three children we're really concerned about. What do you suggest?"

"Love her," Covey replied.

"I told you; the feeling just isn't there anymore."

"Love her," Covey said.

"You don't understand. The feeling of love just isn't there."

"Then love her! If the feeling isn't there, that's a good reason to love her."

"But how do you love when you don't love?"

"My friend, love is a verb."

(This part really hit me.) He said, **"Love—the feeling—is the fruit of love, the verb.** So, love her. Serve her. Sacrifice for her. Listen to her. Empathize with her. Appreciate her. Affirm her. Are you willing to do that?"

So if you want to feel love, it comes from doing the things that true love inspires.

That sounds simple and natural. Right? But here's where this simple truth gets a little more complicated.

Think of the things that true love might inspire you to do for your partner. You love her. You want to comfort her and show her appreciation. You want to do something sweet and thoughtful for her. A nice dinner out? An unexpected gift? A weekend away? Flowers on the counter? Those are great and natural ideas.

Unless…

What if your partner is struggling to stay on a particular diet? That well-intended invitation to dinner out could force her into an awkward place. She'd either have to decline your kindhearted gesture or say yes to dinner and break her diet—her commitment and promise to herself.

What if your partner is worried about your budget? What if she is really, truly grateful for the unexpected gift, but is going to worry all month that bills might not get paid?

What if your partner worked all week and has been looking forward to a warm shower, some cozy pajamas, closed blinds, and some relaxation at home this weekend? What if she just wanted to make sure that the chores were all done for the upcoming week, so she didn't feel so stressed out? What if that weekend away, although beautiful and romantic and well earned, is the exact opposite of what she needs and wants? Maybe your partner is on a diet AND is worried about the budget, AND is exhausted from a brutal week filled with responsibilities?

Here's where true love (love, the verb) comes in. In order to truly love her, you need to listen. You need to check in. You need to stay engaged, guys. Know your partner. Know her ups and downs. Know what makes her frustrated and angry. Know what brings her peace and smiles and laughter. To know her is to love her. Love...the verb. Know what she needs and wants. Share what you need with her...from her...without inhibition. Your openness with her will encourage openness with you, which might lead to you to a Friday evening:

- Cooking a healthy dinner at home that supports your partner's nutritional goals...

- Making sure her favorite pajamas are not only clean but toasty fresh from the dryer...

- Filling a warm and bubbly tub or running a steamy shower for her to relax in...

- Giving her a card you made (not bought) that's filled with words of sincere love and appreciation...

- Presenting her with some flowers or a small treat that didn't break the bank like a weekend away would have.

The dinner will be eaten. The pajamas get dirty and go back in the laundry. The flowers will die. But the way you made her feel never will, because you showed her that she matters. You loved her. You showed her that you love her enough to simply pay attention and to put her goals and fears and thoughts and emotions first. You were listening. You love her.

Some say that true love takes work. I don't believe that to be the case unless you're considering "labors of love" to be work. Yes, it can take sacrifice. Maybe you wanted to go away over the weekend. Maybe you wanted to go out to dinner. Maybe you wanted to buy her an expensive gift. So share your desires and plans and disappointments with her open-ly. There will be a time and a place for that. But the love you feel on this particular Friday night will certainly be true, and it will certainly be the fruit of the respect, consideration, and love that you gave.

In my experience, the "work" that you put into that peaceful, relax-ing Friday night isn't work at all. It's a gift! The "sacrifice" feels good. The whole evening, although it took planning and execution, was effortless, and the love was true. It will be remembered, and often reciprocated in its own way in its own time.

Love, the noun. It's the most beautiful thing I've ever known. If it's missing, if it's fading...then take action and love!

Love is a verb.

I love you guys, and I feel loved.

Five Words

23

The Selfish Irony of the Golden Rule

Hey guys, it's Dad.

Last night, listening to an audiobook, I heard a comment about the Golden Rule, and it kinda started to bug me! I didn't really understand why. It took me a moment to figure it out. It's something that we talked a bit about recently, so I thought I'd share my thoughts.

The author I was listening to was discussing the relationship between actions and consequences; between behaviors and expectations. But, when he encouraged us to "Follow the Golden Rule," something didn't sit right with me. "Doing the right thing" isn't that simple of an idea, is it? There's got to be more behind it. Right?

Yes. There is. There's a lot more behind it.

So in the blurry hours in the middle of the night, I thought long and hard about it. The Golden Rule has served us well for hundreds of years, if not thousands, but it has surely seen its better days. I mean, centuries ago, we walked everywhere, then we used horses to get from point A to point B, then wagons and carriages. Now we drive electric cars. Sometimes it's just time to move forward; it's time to evolve, and this is one of those times.

With some insight and some foresight...we can do better. Yep. Today is the day to put that old cliche in a scrapbook, then find something better; something further down the path of social evolution.

On the surface, the title of this post likely appears to contradict itself. How could the Golden Rule possibly be selfish? Isn't it the opposite of selfish?

Nope! It's selfish.

In fact, it's completely selfish—100% self-centered, by definition! It puts "I" at the center of "Others."

As a teacher, a coach, and a dad, I know that we don't all have the same needs and wants. What each of us perceives as a reward (our wants and wishes) varies greatly from person to person. While one person wants a new iPhone, another wants a new pair of basketball shoes, while a third wants a weekend away, camping and fishing with grandma and grandpa. This is not news to anyone. It's part of what makes each of us unique. But I think we've forgotten to pay attention to it. Variety is truly the spice of life, right?

With this idea in mind, why would I ever want to "Treat others the way that I want to be treated"? I shouldn't! Boom. Done! Put it in the scrapbook!

Next!

So what's next? What's better than the Golden Rule? Let's call it the Platinum Rule:

"Treat others the way that they want to be treated."

Now take a good look at the depth and breadth of changes, in both behavior and mindset, that this change of views forces us to adopt.

The Platinum Rule takes the focus off of "us" and puts it on "them," where it belongs. It's no longer on "I." It's on "others."

There's a kinda sad trend that's been happening over the years. With each passing generation, it feels as though we're becoming more self-centered. It is clear that in order to create the next significant step in our social growth or evolution we'll need to focus on the needs, wants, and feelings of others. With this new mindset, we can more easily see the necessary changes that the title of this post is pointing to—the unintended and ironically selfish nature of the Golden Rule.

Now, looking back, the Golden Rule seems almost laughable.

Ahhhhh...but it gets better.

Among a growing sea of faces buried in digital devices, we're growing disconnected from each other. This disconnection isn't just a change in how we interact, it's becoming divisive. It's separating us. Check the news tonight. How are we doing? Like...maybe we're getting a C- in "Life," if we're lucky.

This disconnection with each other is rapidly becoming a bit of a crisis. The comfort that we've taken in isolating ourselves is creating alarming increases in the rates and levels of depression, stress, illness, addiction, obesity, and loneliness. Sadly, all of these conditions play very nicely together. One often leads to another.

So where's the knight in shining armor? Who's going to save us from this dark, downward spiral?

It's not a "who"...but a "what."

That "what" is connection—reconnection.

Now here's the hook.

Built into the Platinum Rule (like we snuck it in while nobody was watching) is an inherent necessity to reconnect. In order to do what's right for others, we first have to get to know them! How can I possibly know how others want to be treated, what makes them smile, what brings them peace if I don't really know them at all? I have to know them and understand them, and the only way to do that…is to connect.

So…that's it! Out with the old and in with the new! Let's start making eye contact. Let's start connecting and reconnecting. Then, let's start treating people the way that they want to be treated.

I love you guys.

Five Words

Love, Dad

24

What's More Honest than Honesty?

Hey guys! It's Dad.

When we think about being honest, being truthful, we can see the inseparable consequence to honesty: trust! When you're honest, day in and day out, you're going to be trusted. In the same way...if you want to be liked, be likable. If you want to be loved, be loveable. If you want friends, be friendly. If you want to be trusted, be trustworthy. Be honest. Right? But there's a step beyond honesty that will get you there quicker. Like so many timeless truths...this one is simple. It may not always be easy, but it's simple, and it's a law as real as the laws of physics.

Being forthcoming is better than "telling the truth," in the same way that interdependence is better than independence. Telling the truth is like doing a really good job but not quite finishing it. There's more. It's why (if we're in court, under oath) we're asked to swear to tell the truth, the whole truth, and nothing but the truth.

In our lives, our jobs, our relationships, we can do good things, we can do bad things, or we can do nothing. Looking on the surface, good is good, bad is bad...but doing nothing? That's harmless. Right? Well sometimes it's harmless. Sometimes it's not. And c'mon...is "harmless" what we're shooting for? I think we should set the bar a little higher than that.

Sometimes doing nothing is harmless. Sometimes it's a crime! Yep! You can get in serious trouble for *not* doing something. Crimes can be an act (doing something bad like stealing or hurting someone). But crimes can also be an omission. Sometimes it's called negligence. Sometimes it's just called an omission. When a law specifically requires someone to take action, "I didn't do any harm" is not enough to keep you out of trouble. For example: Not putting out your campfire. Not giving adequate care to a child or an ailing parent. An on-duty police officer not helping someone in danger. Not paying our taxes, etc.

In a similar way, I see that "telling the truth" is always the right thing to do. Yes, sometimes we have to be tactful, sensitive, and aware when we speak the truth. But there's a small step beyond just telling the truth that really, truly matters. It's called being forthcoming.

Honesty isn't enough to bring you the life, the successes, and the relationships that you deserve. Be forthcoming and have integrity.

Love, Dad.

25

The Path to Equality
Must Pass through Equity

Lots of folks don't seem to appreciate the subtle yet significant differences between equity and equality. These two terms are not just overused and underappreciated, but they're often thrown around as if they share the same meaning. However, unless or until we recognize that we can't have the prior without the latter, our road to true social equality is going to be far longer and far more painful than it needs to be.

Just as the universe continues to expand, one way or another we'll reach equality. It's inevitable. It's in our makeup. We can either do it the hard way or the easy way. There are countless analogies we could use to help differentiate the meaning of these two words—equality and equity—but these are the ones I've used to help my students understand:

- If someone is choking, we may need to perform the Heimlich maneuver on them. We don't perform the Heimlich on everyone in the room.

- When a child has been neglected and abused, we provide love, stability, and additional support. We don't provide additional support for every child.

- When someone is ill, we don't provide medical support to everyone. We provide additional medical support only to those who are ill.

- When people lose their way; when they're not living in alignment with their values, we provide clarity and guidance to help them find their voice, their purpose, a new direction. We don't do the same for those who are thriving. They receive different nurturing, support, and guidance.

But how does that help us as individuals and as a society?

It's only after we help the person who's choking; after we've provided additional support; after we've provided medical care to those who need it and redirected those who've strayed, that we will be closer to true equality. The people who needed additional support now have a better chance and are better equipped to leverage the opportunities that present themselves throughout their lives. Free tickets to a Lakers game don't help if the recipient of the free tickets doesn't have the means to get to the game.

We just can't achieve true equality without first providing equity. We, societally, have to provide additional support to those who've been mistreated, neglected, marginalized, and abused.

BUT…before that, **we must earn their trust.**

It might take weeks or months or years to earn trust. Truthfully, in terms of one population learning to trust another…it is likely to take generations. But during that trust-building/rebuilding process we cannot waver in our support; not for an instant.

As with a child who has been repeatedly neglected and abused; whose hopes have been repeatedly dashed; whose sadness and tears have been replaced with anger and fear because her tears have dried, this will take time. It will take compassion and patience and faith and love, beyond anything we've seen before. We've got to listen. We've got to sympathize. We've got to be patient and forgiving.

Like an animal that has been abused, we have to understand that when they bite us (and they will) our commitment cannot falter We need to love them—love, the verb. We need to do those things that we do for the people we love most. But one lapse—just a single lapse in love...in caring...one break in listening, a single instance of losing focus or patience—can bring us right back to the starting line. We can prove them right—that we don't really care. Not only will that send us right back to the starting line...it can move the starting line back even farther.

This IS the path; the path that we created.

This is on us.

Let's give love.

Let's earn trust.

Let's cross the finish line together, arm in arm, looking back to ensure that no one is ever left behind again.

I love you guys.

Five Words

Love, Dad

26

How to Be...Happy?

Hi guys! It's Dad!

Today I'm writing to you about happiness. More specifically, I'm writing about creating—or even simpler than that, allowing—happiness in your lives.

Sometimes we find ourselves feeling unhappy, and sometimes that feeling can become almost crippling. We can feel so overcome with sadness that we can't seem to shake it, even when we're in a safe, love-filled environment. This feeling of unhappiness can be caused by so many things. It can be caused by the way that someone treated us. It can be the result of an unfortunate event or circumstance. Sometimes it can even be caused by ourselves. As weird as that may seem, it's true! Sadness can be self-inflicted. Maybe we've behaved in a way that isn't in alignment with our values. That causes an ugly, heavy feeling inside that we call "guilt." Even weirder than that is the fact that sadness sometimes interrupts our day and we don't have any idea why we're feeling so sad in the first place. But those feelings are real, and they hurt just the same.

This post is a simple reminder of just how simple it can be to get yourselves out of that sad place; that unhappy place where we all find ourselves from time to time.

A little while back, I read a story from an ancient book of wisdom. It spoke of a time when an old wise man used the same ideas that I'm going to share with you to help a king find true and timeless happiness. The story went something like this:

A wealthy and powerful king had everything he could ever ask for, but he was still often unhappy. He had power, riches, and comfort— but was often feeling sad, lost, unfulfilled, and without purpose. He sought the guidance of an old wise man with the hope that he could help the king find happiness.

The king said to the wise man, "I just don't know what to do in order to find happiness. I have everything that anyone could ever ask for, yet I'm sad. Will you please help me be happy? What does it take to be happy?"

The wise man gave a single word response to the king. "Help."

To that, the king replied, "Help? Do you need help?"

"No," said the wise man. "Help. That's the path to happiness."

The king shouted back, "That's it? That's the wisdom you're going to bestow upon me, the king? Help? Help whom, old man?"

The wise man said, without hesitation, "Whom you are with."

And to that, the king asked, "When do I do that? When do I 'help those whom I am with'?"

The old man said, "Now. Help...whom you are with...now. That is the key to happiness."

The good news is that the path to real, lasting, rich, and fulfilling happiness is actually that simple. Help, whom you are with, now—in the moment you are in. That's pretty easy, right?

No. Simple doesn't necessarily mean easy. Carrying forty cases of bottled water from the truck to the garage is simple, but it's not very easy. But the more you do it...the easier it gets. With practice, you'll grow the muscles necessary to carry those heavy cases of water more easily. Being happy; living happily works in much the same way. Just like carrying heavy cases of water...it will get easier the more you practice it.

OK...step by step...this is how it's done. This is how you can interrupt your feelings and be happy in those moments when you're down.

Think for a moment about what makes you feel joyful, or cheerful. Is it laughter? Is it gratitude for all you have? Is it when someone gives you a compliment or makes you feel good about yourself? Is it when someone cares enough about you to help you do something that you need to get done?

Instead of waiting for that to happen to you, turn what makes you feel happiness into actions that you can take to create happiness in someone else.

Go do those things for someone else! Make someone laugh. Give them a compliment. Ask them a question about themselves, then give them your undivided attention while you listen. Do random acts of kindness—such as holding a door open for someone, bringing your neighbor's trash cans up from the street, offering to help someone with a chore, or simply offering a smile. Just give of yourself; be of service to others. You'll see for yourselves that almost immediately after you do these things...you start feeling happy.

There's real science behind all of this "happiness" stuff too. It's not just talk. It's about refocusing your attention (taking your mind off of your own heartache and focusing it on something positive), and creating physical movement and motion (positive motions create positive emotions, like when we go to the gym and we feel so great afterward), as well as the simple joy that comes as a natural reward for doing something good for someone else.

But there are even more things that will physically, mentally, and emotionally bring you happiness.

Make sure that you've given your body the nutrition to function properly. Stop and think, *"Have I eaten strong foods today…or junky, weak foods?"*

Ask yourself if you're sufficiently hydrated. Have you had enough water or fresh fruit juices today?

Do you feel rested? Did you allow yourself to fall asleep peacefully last night, or did you fall asleep to a YouTube video or video game? And did you get enough hours of sleep?

Are you feeling sluggish or lethargic? Sometimes we call ourselves "bored" when we're actually feeling something called "lethargy." Did you get at least 60 minutes of hard, physical activity today? Without consistent exercise you'll ultimately start to feel down.

Have you learned something today? Did you exercise your brain today through reading, inquiring, or creating?

Finally, have you spent time today focusing on all of the things that we've been blessed with? Have you allowed yourself to simply be still for a few moments and actually feel gratitude? Have you told God, the universe, the people around you that you're grateful for your health, your home, and all of your blessings?

Ultimately, you don't have to know how it all works...just know that it works. I promise to you both that I uses these strategies every day; sometimes all day! Do you know anyone consistently happier than I am? It works, boys.

So, if you're feeling off track, down, depressed...just make sure that you're ticking all of the boxes. OK?

I love you, boys.

Five Words

Dad

27

Fight Fire with Fire? Let's Not!

"An eye for an eye and the whole world goes blind."

— GANDHI

Hey guys! It's Dad.

You know the very high standard of behavior that I expect from you guys, and you rise to that standard every day. Your actions embody these two simple ideas: Be gentlemen and be humble.

I know that sometimes it isn't easy, but you're doing a fantastic job, especially under the circumstances. That said, if I had to add a third behavior to the list it would be this…

Be loving.

Recently we learned of a tragedy that ended with a young girl taking her own life. My understanding is that she was being relentlessly bullied and she just couldn't cope with the pain anymore. I could see how hard that was on you, Michael. Buddy, I know that this touched you in a powerful way. It should. When I watched those tears well up in your eyes and you gave me a long hug, I saw another piece of innocence being washed from your big, beautiful heart. I'm so sorry.

The thought of anyone, much less a child, enduring so much emotional pain for so long completely breaks my heart. That heartache inspired me to write this post.

There's a commonly used quote; a cliché really, with a bit of a 'tough-guy' mentality, that I believe is both misunderstood and misused when it comes to dealing with difficult and challenging times.

"Fight fire with fire!"

More or less, it means that if someone does wrong by you, give 'em a taste of their own medicine. If someone shoves you…shove 'em back! If someone hurts your feelings…hurt 'em back! If someone hates you… hate 'em back.

However, the truth is—at least as I've experienced it in my life—this is usually, if not always, the wrong response to any challenging situation. In fact, it's not a response at all. It's a reaction rooted in pain, fear, or anger. These emotions don't often lead to healthy, helpful, or well-thought-out responses.

Think about that phrase for a moment. "Fight fire with fire!" Granted, in an action film, it sure sounds tough, but think again! If there's a fire…and you add more fire, it just makes…a bigger fire. If someone's being violent, it just introduces more violence. If people are talking trash…it creates more trash!

It might sound kind of funny at first, almost sarcastic, but I prefer to say, "Fight fire with water!" Now doesn't that make more sense?

Let this next bit sink in for a moment.

About 20 years ago the world lost a truly beautiful human being. Her name was Mother Teresa. She did amazing things; peaceful things for all of humankind. In fact, she won the Nobel Peace Prize and was formally recognized by the church as a saint! Well, I recently learned something fascinating about her, her integrity, and her effectiveness. It's so simple I think we'd miss it if I didn't point it out.

In all of her efforts to bring peace into war-torn areas of the world, Mother Teresa never attended a single anti-war rally. Not once! Why not? Isn't she supposed to help bring peace? Isn't war where her attention and focus would best serve us? But she didn't support those events because the focus was on war. She thought, "How can you stop war when you're focusing on war?" Instead, this saint of a lady spoke at countless peace rallies. She focused her time and efforts on promoting peace...not ending war.

Once asked, "How is it that you never seem to judge anyone who comes to you?" She responded, "I never judge anyone because it doesn't allow me the time to love them."

That might seem like a trivial difference, focusing on what we want as opposed to stopping what we don't want. But it is a powerful example of the point that I hope you guys take away from this message. The point is simply this: We don't need to fight to win a war. We can do the opposite of fight, which is to love. We can be the water to the fire.

Jesus once said, "...love your enemies, do good to those who hate you, bless those who curse you, pray for those who mistreat you." He didn't say that this would be easy. I wish he did. But he said that this is the way to peaceful living.

I remember sharing with you, a while back, how Lance Armstrong, that Tour de France guy, lied and cheated and threatened and manipulated thousands of people throughout his career, just so he could win. But, as they always do, his lies caught up with him a few years ago; and when they did, literally hundreds of millions of people hated him. Imagine that: hundreds of millions of people! They absolutely despised him. People threatened him and his family. People bullied his kids. People had so much rage and pain. Even many years later people still held onto that hatred and pain.

Not long ago, while Armstrong was waiting for a taxi near a brewpub in Colorado, a group of people at a restaurant started screaming horrible things at him; vile, horrible things. He didn't know them, and they didn't know him, but they just kept screaming at him. Lance's reaction could have been to return to his old ways of threats and violence and power and manipulation. But what he actually did was amazing and inspiring.

Lance didn't get angry or violent. He didn't fight fire with fire. Instead, as the taxi drove away, he called the restaurant manager on the phone and told the manager what happened. As the manager was apologizing for the behavior of the restaurant's guests, Lance interrupted. He gave the manager his credit card number and said, "I'd like to pay for all of their food and drinks. All of them. So please go pay their bills. Then… tell them that I love them."

Over the past several years Lance could have heard the cries and criticisms of thousands of hurting and angry people and just held onto 'em. He could have let them bring him down, to a dark, dark place. But he searched for answers and for guidance and for growth and he fought through.

We will never know how the angry crowd at the brewpub felt after Lance's kind and loving gesture, but I'd be willing to bet that at least one, if not all of them, grew up a little bit that day. We'll never know for sure, but what I do know is how much better Lance must have felt by offering love and support instead of anger and violence. He chose to fight fire with water. He fought pain and anger with love…and this time…he really won.

I wish that I could tell you that the world is great, and that people are kind, but I can't. You're going to feel the sting of the jagged words of hurtful, hurt-full people. What I did feel compelled to do though, is to make sure that you know that you'll be fine.

I encourage you to be willing to pause in the moment…take a breath, then fight fire with water, fight violence with peace, and fight hate with love. It works, guys. I promise.

Be Gentlemen. Be Humble. Be Loving.

Five Words.

I love you,

Dad.

28

How to Be the Very Best Friend

Hey guys! It's Dad.

This morning I remembered (OK, I didn't remember; my phone reminded me) that it was one of my friend's birthdays. We're pretty close friends, so I called him up to say hello and wish him well. Later, as I was reading over the posts from others on his social media pages, I saw something that I'd seen countless times before, but it never bothered me...until today.

Today I saw a post that simply said, "HBD." Initially, I didn't even really know what it meant. I looked for a response from my friend to see if I could figure it out, but there wasn't one. My buddy "liked" the "HBD" comment, but he still didn't give a response. Then it hit me... HBD! Happy Birthday! When I figured it out, I unconsciously rolled my eyes back and shook my head.

Why did that post upset me? Maybe it didn't really upset me; I just felt disappointed, let down.

We have become so obsessed with efficiency (doing things quickly and with little effort) that I'm afraid that we're all getting through our lives efficiently instead of effectively—happily.

We fast-forward our movies, our TV shows, and even our meals. We're starting to fast-forward our entire lives! We've become so consumed that we've forgotten how to slow down and simply live happily—effectively.

There's a huge difference between effective and efficient. We need to be effective in our relationships, not efficient. Let me explain. Being effective means to produce the highest quality result. That's what we want for our friendships: High quality friends. Think about it for a minute. Do you want your relationships to be efficient (quick and with little effort)? At what point would you want your friends to be "efficient" with you? Where should they cut corners to save time in terms of your friendship? I have very few true friends. But my friends are the very best friends I could ever have, and they matter to me. How they feel matters to me.

Forgive my harshness, but the sender of this thoughtless, emotionless, lazy-man's way to send a birthday wish was either A) so busy that he couldn't be bothered to spend twenty seconds of his valuable time to write a kind, well-thought-out, sincere and effective birthday wish, or B) he didn't actually care about my friend in the first place.

So, here's my question: If you're too busy, don't care, or you're too lazy, why say anything at all? It's not a requirement! You don't need to send a birthday wish. It's likely that nobody would have missed it if you didn't. Imagine what my friend felt on his birthday, when he read "HBD" on his timeline (I bet there were 20 or more identical posts). He probably felt nothing at all, right? So, the birthday wish was ineffective. Now imagine if he saw this on his timeline:

"JOHNNY C!!!!! Happy Birthday! Man, you're 43 now! Crazy how time goes by so fast. I'm 50 now. FIFTY! Feelin' great though, and I hope you are too. I just wanted to send you a quick note letting you know that I was thinking about you, and I wanted to wish you a happy birthday today. I hope you, your bride, and your kiddos have a great time celebrating! Drop me a line if

you're ever out this way, OK? We'll go grab a burrito down the street and get caught up! Again, HAPPY BIRTHDAY! Chat soon!"

There! See? That took just a little under ninety seconds to type out. Less than two minutes!

I know, I know. *"But I've got 1,462 friends on Facebook and it would take me all day to send out sincere birthday wishes. It's just so much easier to use abbreviations."*

Yep, it is. It's so much easier.

Now, I'm not here to tell you that nobody has 1,462 friends, but… but yes, I guess I sort of am. We don't have enough hours in our lives to give ourselves and our love to that many TRUE friends. So, if you can't be bothered to even spell out two simple words, only to replace them with three initials, perhaps it's better that you don't say anything at all. It's funny…Happy Birthday is actually only two words, so wouldn't the abbreviation simply be "HB" in the first place? Heck, that would even save 33% more time by dropping the "D".

When we're dealing with people, our goal should never be "efficiency." It needs to be "effectiveness." "HBD" isn't going to cut it, and neither is a response of "TY."

So how can I be effective in my relationships; in my friendships? Well, just like we have to do in life, we have to be present; we have to live in the moment with our relationships in order to be effective. We have to show a sense of authenticity and vulnerability. We need make the time and take the time to communicate our intended messages.

In today's day and age of shortcuts, life hacking strategies, laziness, and narcissism (that means really only being interested in yourself) you and I actually have a real opportunity to stand out. We can stand out as the very best of friends, a loving brother, cousin, or child. All we have to do is take a few extra moments away from ourselves and give those few moments, give that love, to a few people that mean the most to us. You can give those moments to someone who needs them. You can lend an ear to a friend that wants to share. You can stop for a moment and think of a happy memory, then reach out to the people you were with at that happy time and say thank you.

When I was really young, your Papa Jim told me that God gave us two ears and one mouth so that we would listen more than we speak. THAT is a beautiful lesson in effectiveness. I'm no expert, but it has served me well in my relationships at home, with friends, at school, with clients, and on and on.

Don't be quick with your friends, be excellent with your friends.

Show an interest in them. Ask them questions, then listen...with the sole purpose being to understand their excitement, their pain, or their fears. Then, once you understand how they're feeling, lean on the Platinum Rule. Treat them as they wish to be treated. Treat them in a way that would make them appreciate your attention. Comfort them, laugh with them, celebrate with them; celebrate for them.

If you do this, you will have more true friends than you can possibly imagine, but not so many that you have to wish them all a "HBD."

Five Words

Love, Dad

29

Don't "Spend" Your Time. Invest It.

I've been hurt, and I've been lied to. I've been stolen from, and I've been betrayed. I've been abused, deceived, and intentionally misled... and I'm grateful for every last bit of it. Ironically, it has ushered peace into my life.

I know. I know. I can hear the sarcastic eyerolls and head shakes already. "Oh sure! I'm SOOO happy that I got in that car accident!" and "I love that my boyfriend cheated on me with my best friend!" and on and on. Grumble away, but I don't think it's gonna help. I'm not here to spout clichés like "Everything happens for a reason." I won't tell you that everything bad that happens to you is actually good. But I will tell you that everything bad that happens to you can be empowering...and it should be.

We don't grow during easy times. We grow—physically, mentally, spiritually, emotionally—during challenging times. The harder the challenge that we push through, the greater the growth. I'm grateful for the courage and the humility, the strength and the vulnerability, and the patience and understanding that this life has taught me.

In the beginning of Eckhart Tolle's book, *A New Earth*, he wrote:

"If the history of humanity were the clinical case history of a single human being, the diagnosis would have to be: chronic paranoid delusions, a pathological propensity to commit murder and acts of extreme violence and cruelty against his perceived 'enemies'—his own unconsciousness projected outward. Criminally insane, with a few brief lucid intervals."

That's a diagnosis that's not only hard to stomach, but sadly accurate. So, let's breathe for a moment. Let's lower our expectations. Remember that all disappointment lives in the gap between an occurrence and our often arbitrarily attached expectations of what that occurrence "should have been." The idea that we will all, in all of our dysfunction, somehow miraculously grow into fully functioning, well-balanced, compassionate adults, with no baggage, no unhealthy coping strategies, no ill-conceived notions of what should or shouldn't be—well...it's a pretty lofty expectation. If, like me, you find yourself not always living up to your own expectations (or others' expectations of you), take a deep breath, smile, then breathe again. You're not alone.

That sort-of "who we are" part of us is subject to so many outside influences. Our emotions are like buoys bobbing around in stormy seas. Day after day, life after life, we spend so much energy and so many emotions on worries, regrets, resentments, fears, and animosity. I'm here to ask you...to implore you...to never spend another moment as long as you live.

Wait! That doesn't even make sense! "Don't spend another moment?"

Hear me out. I promise, it makes sense; deep, peaceful sense.

When it comes to money, we can spend it or we can invest it. We can spend money on junk food with no nutritional value, or we can invest the same amount of money into our health and wellbeing. Like every investment, the returns won't be immediate. But run this little junk food vs. nutrition scenario down the road a few years and see what happens. Like investing money, it won't take long until those two different paths (one conscious and one unconscious) lead us in two dramatically different directions:

Path 1: Spend your money on fast food and snacks. Tasty? Heck yes! Easy? Very. But this isn't a guess; it's a fact: If you're living on junk food, you will eventually start to age prematurely, and you'll feel weak, sick, lethargic, and depressed. Consider this for a moment: We live in a time when people are both morbidly obese **and** starving to death at the same time.

Path 2: Invest wisely in your nutrition. If you are living on foods that are nutrient-rich, foods that have actually seen the soil, you'll eventually start to feel stronger, more vibrant, more creative and productive, happier, and more optimistic. Again, this isn't a guess. Like gravity, it's a law. There's no way around it. We cannot detach the consequence from the action.

There's a significant fundamental difference between spending and investing. Don't spend your money on food. Invest in your health. Invest in your physical body and your mental wellness.

But the same needs to be said about our emotions and energy. We shouldn't be "spending" them when we can invest them, wisely, if we know how.

Before we go down that rabbit hole though, we need to acknowledge one painful truth. We don't typically invest our emotions or even "spend" them. Our emotions spend us. Much like thinking—thinking just happens whether we want it to or not. Our emotions are often doing the same thing. They tend to just chew us up and spit us out on a whim. Incessant thinking hijacks our brains, while unhealthy and undermining emotions run amok in our hearts.

Most of us are at the beck and call of our emotions. They say, "JUMP!" We say, "How high?" They say, "Be anxious!" We say, "Sir! Yes sir!" They say, "Be resentful!!!" We say, "I already am!"

Sometimes, if not all the time (and I'm guilty as charged), if we check our breathing and check our tension—the tension we hold in our shoulders, in our neck, in our jaws, our brow, our tongue pushed into the roof of our mouths—we'll notice that our emotions are being spent every waking moment, and we seemingly have no control over it. But can we stop spending and start investing our emotions?

Our emotions are really "us." They are the essence of who we are. We aren't our bodies. We are the intangible qualities inside and even around our bodies. The highest tech medical imaging equipment can't see "us." An MRI will show soft tissue damage, but it won't find love. An x-ray shows broken bones, but it will never show betrayal or a broken heart. A blood test won't reveal our dreams and aspirations. Those feelings and emotions are who we are. But how do we keep that part of "us" healthy? If you're like me, even as a churchgoer, it took trauma and heartache to finally discover how.

We have to learn.

If we study, and learn, and even pay people to look after our finances, we learn how to save and how to invest. But who teaches us how to save ourselves? Where are our teachers, mentors, and coaches that help us learn how to invest our emotions in a healthy way?

Explore, and you will find the answers. I promise. They are out there. And in this day and age, they're all literally at your fingertips. The teachers and mentors, whether it's in the form of a podcast or the Rig Veda written some 3,500 years ago, they're out there, and they always have been. But unless we notice that we need guidance—we need a mentor, a scripture, a resource—we won't go exploring. We need to recognize that we're lost first.

I heard a quote from a Netflix film called *I'm Not Your Guru*. It said, "If you're gonna blame, blame fairly." This idea just illustrates the idea that if you're going to hold resentment against someone for cheating on you, then you have to thank them for giving you strength and independence. If you're going to beat yourself up over something you did in your past, then be grateful for learning how to forgive yourself, or at least realizing that you can. If someone bullied you, thank them for pushing you to a place that was so uncomfortable that you had to grow from it. Find the good. Use the good...yes, the cheesy "silver lining" positives that come from your most painful and trying experiences. Let them empower you. Let them be the fuel you'll need in order to grow, the motivation you'll need in order to persevere, and ultimately the knock from your comfortable perch that helps you find your voice; your purpose.

Your purpose will always outlast your motivation.

When we talk about money, there's no bigger truth than, "You can't take it with you." Well, the same can be said about our emotions. There are 60 minutes in every hour. If someone steals five of them from you, how many more minutes will you spend hating and resenting and wishing that things were different? How many of those minutes are you going to spend in the past versus how many are you going to invest in your future and in your peace?

Brené Brown said, "You are imperfect, you are wired for struggle, but you are worthy of love and belonging."

You deserve to be happy. YOU deserve to be happy. Invest your emotions. Don't spend 'em. And if you have to blame...blame fairly.

Hugs,

Dad

30

We'll Always Find What We're Looking For

"We don't see things as they are, we can only see things as we are."
– The Talmud

As I continue to grow and to practice what I preach to my students and to my own sons, the more I'm convinced that we see what we want to see and what we have been conditioned to see, even if it's unpleasant.

We're unconsciously looking for more of what we're accustomed to seeing. Sometimes we can even hear ourselves perpetuating our circumstances and emotions. "Oh my gosh! I have the worst luck!" or "How come I can't just meet a guy who isn't a jerk?" These thoughts and our self-talk help us to justify our current life circumstances. We repeat it. Then...we share it. We manifest it and bring more of it into our lives.

But what if, instead of doing that unconsciously, we consciously looked for something different, something better? What if we made an effort to see the good in people, to see the service, to appreciate the perseverance of the amazing people who surround us every day...then we shared that? Wouldn't we, in turn, unconsciously start to see and share more and more of that? More and more of the good?

If we all tried, if we made it our homework...our responsibility... couldn't we find the good, the love, and the inspiration so frequently that we stop empowering the bad? Couldn't we be so relentless in our awareness of the good that the bad and the ugly no longer have room to flourish? I think we can. I think I have.

While out for a run I came across a massive, refrigerator-sized cardboard box that someone had discarded in the middle of a busy suburban street. Initially I felt a little twinge of anger, disappointment, and I even felt disrespected. It's my neighborhood. Then, as I ran closer to it to pull it to the side of the road, that twinge turned into a twinkle. As I got closer all I could see was what I try to see all the time...in everything and in everyone.

I saw love.

In fact, it was literally cut by an industrial machine right into the side of this massive chunk of garbage. Yeah, I'm sure that engineers designed it as a handle, but I saw something else... because it's what I want to see, because it's what I look for.

Years ago, I'd have held onto that disappointing feeling and let it nag at me for a bit. I probably would have asked a neighbor, "Did you see that big box in the middle of the road? What the heck? How could somebody...blah blah blah." Sharing the negative. But I've trained myself and broken that bad, seemingly innate habit. Now, I hold onto love. I hold onto the good that I see...I share that. In fact, I try to only share that...and I let it crowd out the bad and the ugly.

It takes practice to recognize the negativity that stealthily creeps into us while we're unaware. We just need to become aware. That ugly feeling isn't pleasant, so recognize it as a sign, a message to yourself to look for something else; something good.

Look for love, and if you can't find it...create it, then leave it for someone else to find.

I hope today brings you love. Actually...I hope that you see the love that today already brought, then I hope you share it.

Hugs,

Dad

31

Let's Burn the Boats

"The only things I'll ever regret are things I didn't do.
In the end, that's what we'll mourn.
The paths we didn't take.
The people we didn't touch."
– Scott Spencer, American Author

Hey guys.

You know that I've written about risk and regret. I've studied it. I've lived it from both sides of the fence. I'm almost hyper-aware of the importance of just going for it. There's so much good to come from it, and almost always such little at risk.

But even with that conscious mindfulness, sometimes anxieties and fears still find a way to creep in. Like water seeping through the cracks in the hull of a ship, we need to be mindful that it's there or we'll end up spending our lives bailing water, simply trying to stay afloat. Before we know it, we'll reach the end of this journey having missed every coastline, every sunrise, every sunset, and every mile and every smile in between.

Below is a story that was shared with me by a professor of mine. His intention was to instill in us an urgency to act. No hesitation. No doubt. Just go all in, in an effort to reach your goals and dreams.

Burning the Boats

As the legend goes, Spanish conquistador Hernán Cortés issued a frightening order to his soldiers as they attempted, yet again, to overthrow the Aztecs.

Cortés, a great warrior in his own right, had to make a decision which would ensure his success on the battlefield. He was about to send his army to fight a far superior and more powerful army on their home soil. He loaded his soldiers into boats, sailed to the Aztec empire, and unloaded soldiers and equipment. He then gave the order to sail the ships just offshore to set them ablaze. He told his soldiers before the battle, "You see the boats going up in smoke? That means that we will never leave these shores alive...unless we win! We now have no choice—we win or we perish!"

In 1933, incoming US President Franklin D. Roosevelt said, "...let me assert my firm belief that the only thing we have to fear is...fear itself — nameless, unreasoning, unjustified terror which paralyzes needed efforts to convert retreat into advance." Cortés converted retreat into advance, and you guys can too.

The point my professor was making was that Cortés' level of commitment is the same level of commitment that we should take when pursuing our own dreams. But we don't have to worry about dying in the process. Sure, we might fail. We might lose some money. We might lose a lot! When we're older, we could even lose our homes or our business. But unlike the soldiers that ultimately defeated the Aztecs, we don't have to literally face a win-or-die scenario. We're often just too afraid to go all in. We're afraid of getting it wrong. We're afraid of failure.

You've Still Got a Mulligan

You may not know what a "Mulligan" is in golf, but really, it's a fancy name for a do-over. Basically, if you mess up your shot, the people you're playing with might give you a second chance. Guys, we live in a nation that will always give you a second chance. If your business fails, if you don't graduate, if you go broke, our country has systems built in to help you get back on your feet.

Hank Haney is a golf coach for the pros. I remember him teaching a celebrity how to improve his golf game when he shared an amazing statistic. It really shines a light on the importance that letting go of the fear and giving it your best shot. Haney recorded the percentage of tee shots that his clients hit that landed in the fairway (where you want to be). If they messed up their shots, he gave them a "Mulligan." They got to take another shot. The second shot might have been better, or it could have been worse. Then they would play on. During their next round of golf, he told his clients in advance that they had an extra shot if they needed it. So, if they messed up their shot, they knew they would have a do-over! They didn't need it. The simple knowledge that they had a "safety net," their do-over, changed their unconscious mind and they performed better; not just better...much better! Use your "Mulligan," guys. Go all in! I'll catch you if you fall.

I want you to look at your dreams with a complete lack of inhibition. In a way, I want you to look at your dreams with a complete lack of responsibility. Send it! What have you got to lose if you stumble and fall? What are you giving up if you don't even give yourselves a chance to truly live?

Don't miss the journey. Don't miss a single sunrise or sunset while you're bailing water out of the hull. I promise you'll see storms along the way, but man...the sun looks even brighter after that. Alexander Graham Bell said, "We often look so long and so regretfully upon the closed door that we do not see the one which has opened for us." Push 'em open, guys. Kick 'em open if you have to. At least see what your dreams might bring you.

Don't mourn the things you didn't do, the paths you didn't take, and the people you didn't impact. Let's go! Let's burn our boats.

I love you guys.

Five Words

Love, Dad

32

Searching for Solace

Right now, right this minute, there are unhappy people all over the world. Truth...I try not to think about it. But I care...a lot. We all deserve happiness. Yes. We all do.

People from every race, every age, every creed, living under diverse economic circumstances, are feeling unfulfilled. They're hurt, they have scars from the past, and they fear the future. They have financial problems, health problems, relationship problems. They're losing faith and feeling unfulfilled, fighting to justify the guilt that they feel for squandering the opportunities that they've been given.

They're not weak. They're strong. They are the quiet heroes of their own thankless lives. They're not giving up. They're looking for answers, solutions, a better way, a way out, or simply something...anything...that brings a little joy.

Solace.

They're searching for solace. They hope, they wish, they dream, and they wait. Waking up, day after relentless day, to an unceasing storm of anxieties and obligations, knowing full well that tomorrow will be the same...and tomorrow after that.

I'm sorry to say that the answer, the solution, that solace...it's not out there. It never was and it never will be. We've got to stop looking "out there" for it.

Like so many problems in our lives, it's often not the problem that's the biggest obstacle. It's how we see the problem that trips us up. We need a new point of view. We need to see things as they are and be reminded that it's OK. It's not only OK, but also perfect. It's as it needs to be.

As Albert Einstein said, "We cannot solve our problems with the same thinking we used when we created them."

Recently I was out for an evening run. My body wasn't very happy with me. My run turned into a jog, then a trudge, then a walk. As my pace declined, I found that my thoughts slowly switched from, *"What the heck! Why do I feel like trash today?"* to thinking about how it was possible to be struggling so much yet to be so happy.

My body (or maybe my nutrition) had really let me down. A few chronic aches and pains decided to take center stage again. Concerns about a few members of my extended family were present and very real. But inside, I was happy; legitimately happy. I almost felt guilty, like it was somehow unfair that while so many others are clearly struggling to simply find a single smile in their day, I'm happily "enhancing" the smile lines in my cheeks. I floated through the aches and pains until I got back home. As "tree-hugger" as it sounds, I was literally and figuratively glowing.

That feeling—joy—it's not out there anywhere. Goodness knows I've tried to find it. It's not in a bottle or an activity. It's not found in justice or in karmic retribution. It's inside, and I believe that, in spite of the severity of our unique life circumstances, we can truly be happy anywhere...anytime. We may not know how yet, or believe yet, but it's possible.

Now this way of seeing things, this belief that we can always be happy, and it's up to us...it comes with a built-in cop-out. It sounds very hocus-pocus. It's pretty easy to say, "Alright, Pollyanna! That's about enough garbage for one night!" But even in that, is a fundamental position of "Joy is garbage." It isn't garbage, and we all want it. Every race, every age, every socio-economic group, and every faith. We all want to be happy.

The tough love in me is saying that if we see with new eyes that our misery, our unhappiness, our emptiness, and loneliness is really a choice, then we're wiping away our excuses. For some of us, that's a horrifying prospect. If we accept that we can simply choose to be happy, that means that we could have chosen to be happy all along. We're wiping away our "right to self-pity"...and for some, we'd be wiping away our identity.

"If I don't complain about something, complain about the injustice that I've endured or the conditions with which I live...then nobody will listen. If nobody listens...no one will come and comfort me. Heck, I don't think anyone will even notice me anymore." Those are real feelings for real people all over the world.

Consider the pain and detriment of living in such a cold, hard cage like that. To think that the only attention we might get is pity and sympathy. Not just to think it, but to live it. To build an entire life upon it. I understand it. I've seen it. I think it's tragic.

There's a pretty great little book called It's Never Too Late to Have a Happy Childhood. It truly isn't too late. I'm proof of that myself! Although my childhood was full, overflowing with life. But that doesn't guarantee peace and happiness. Why not? Because happiness comes from inside. All of the boat trips, vacations, video games, and family reunions couldn't bring me happiness. Or maybe they just didn't help me find it.

We've got to be willing to accept the fact that our childhood may be over, but many if not most of us are still carrying around our perspectives from time in our lives. We've gotta stop. Swallowing that truth isn't gonna be easy. But I'm not saying it's gonna be easy. I'm saying it's gonna be worth it. Like heavy bags of luggage you're carrying through the airport, let's put down our baggage and enjoy what's left.

As a teacher and a dad, I'm probably hyperaware of recognizing opportunities to learn, to grow, and to share. As I walked the last half-mile back to my house after a dismal attempt at a run, I wanted to find an effective, engaging way to share with my boys the truth that our happiness, the entire depth of our own happiness, lies inside us. I wanted them to see that joy is always within reach. It's always...within.

My sons have had some growing pains recently. I just wanted them to learn that they don't need to carry those feelings around with them forever. It's healthy to accept things as they are, to hurt, to grieve, to feel let down, and to feel all of the feelings that come to them naturally. But I also want them to learn that those emotions don't make them who they are. Who they are determines what they do with those emotions. Here is what I shared with my sons, one at a time, with quite different responses from each.

The sun had just set when I walked in the door. I said hello to them both, then asked one to come and see me in the kitchen. The curiosity, evident in his body language, seemed to go from "What chores do I have to do?" to "But Dad, I was watching YouTube!"

I asked my younger son to stand in the kitchen, looking out the west-facing kitchen window that reveals the most beautiful southern California sunsets nearly every night. Although the sun was completely gone and it was really dark out, I asked him to look out at the sunset. He furrowed his brown and looked at me like I was stupid (I recognized the look right away). Then I turned off all of the lights in the house. "Can you see it now?" I asked. Again, he gave me the same look. I could hear his thoughts, *"Bruh! The sun went down twenty minutes ago!"* Then I asked him to close his eyes and visualize the sunset we'd just seen.

"Visualize the bright, vibrant colors in the sky. See them right now in your imagination. Even imagine the ocean underneath the sunset if you want. Make it your own vision. Now take a deep breath and just 'be.' Just be in the moment. Soak up the view. Maybe you can hear the waves breaking on the shoreline. Be happy. Don't worry about your schoolwork, the news we'd just received from the family, or anything else. Just be. Imagine the sounds of birds, or maybe the sounds of a harbor with the lines on the sailboats striking their masts." I told him to take another big, deep breath, then let it all out.

"How do you feel, son? Don't think about it…just feel. How do you feel?" I asked.

"Peaceful. Happy. Like I want to go to the beach, Dad," he said.

Then I told him to open his eyes. "Look out the window again, son. Look really hard."

Again, I get back a dismissive glance. "Hang on, buddy. Let me turn the light on for you." I turned the kitchen lights on; bright, white, LED lights. "Now look out there. What do you see?"

"Great! Now I can't see anything at all, Dad," he said.

"Sure you can, buddy! Look harder. You see something! What is it?"

He sighed, "All I can see is me! I can only see my reflection. I can't see past it."

"Isn't that exactly where the happiness was, son? Isn't that where happiness always is? Inside? That vision you had. It only exists in you."

Then, just like that, as I find happens so often, he inadvertently turned our little exercise back on me. "But Dad. That wasn't what I was looking for. I was looking past me, beyond me, out there."

"That's what we all do, buddy. That's what we all do. We look beyond ourselves to find our happiness. We don't need to. It's always within us. It's always only within us."

His breath abruptly halted. His eyebrows raised. His gaze went blank. He blinked his eyes several times and sort of bit his bottom lip. Then took his glasses off and wiped his eyes which had welled up with tears. "I guess we're responsible for our own happiness then. Aren't we? Like it doesn't matter what's going on in our lives, we can choose to be happy... or not happy. It's up to us. Right?"

Too big to cry in front of dad anymore, he wiped his eyes again, put his glasses on, took a few deep breaths as he walked away into the game room.

And where did that leave me on a Tuesday night with an aching body, a dirty kitchen, concerns about the family, and another son to share the exercise with?

Gushing with joy and gratitude. Happy inside.

We...individually and collectively...we've been through a lot. We're going through a lot. We'll continue to go through a lot. It's natural and healthy to search for peace, to search for love, to search for solace. But we've got to stop searching "out there. Beyond myself."

The way we see our past and the world around us is a direct reflection of the world within us. Maybe happiness isn't so far away, and maybe others even see happiness within us that we've never recognized within ourselves.

I hope that you take a look sometime. And if you forget, mired in the thick of things...maybe the next time you see a reflection of yourself in a window...you'll pause for a minute and find a little happiness on the inside that deserves to be seen and felt and nurtured.

It's in you! Can you feel it?

33

Chase Uncertainty. Rest in Certainty.

Hey guys! It's Dad.

You know that I want nothing more for each of you than to see you living a joy filled life. What's kind of crazy though is that most people don't learn how to create joy in their lives until they're much older. I'm hoping that, with a little bit of understanding, I can help you recognize joy in your lives before you're old like Dad! Goodness knows, it took me a long time to be truly happy. But now that I found the way, I want to help you guys cut to the chase and truly start living joy-filled lives!

In Chinese philosophy, Yin and Yang are a sort of graphic representation of how two very different or even opposite forces can work together to create harmony or balance in your life. You've probably seen the symbol for Yin and Yang. It's a black and white design with two sort of swirling shapes that wrap around each other. One is black with a white dot in the middle, and one is white with a black dot, but the amount of black and white within the design is exactly equal. It's perfectly balanced between light and dark. Balance is a key element of any joy-filled life.

The idea for this post came to me when we had just left Ensenada, Mexico. We were on a Disney Cruise. We were playing games, watching movies, eating, laughing a lot, and really feeling pampered. Of course, this was in sharp contrast to Ensenada. You guys had never seen anything like Ensenada before. It was pretty run-down. It was rough-looking. It certainly wasn't the comfortable suburban environment that you are accustomed to with big houses.

We had just gotten back onto the ship, a bit anxious and a bit exhausted, when Jeffrey said, "this is almost like home! Watching *Bizaard-vark* and eating snacks. Just chillin'!"

When we were back on the boat, you knew that you were safe and secure. You were comfortable. You were certain about your surroundings. Even though we were away from home, you had something important; something absolutely vital to a joy-filled life. You had certainty.

When you're home, and you know that you have food in the fridge, clean clothes in your drawers, and a safe warm bed, you know that you're safe. You're certain that you're safe.

This next part is where many folks miss the boat. We all need certainty, but we also need a completely different element in order to find joy. In fact, it's not just different. It's the complete opposite. In order to truly recognize joy, we must experience uncertainty in our lives. We have to "not know." We've got to wonder what's next. We've got to be fearful. We need to feel those chemicals naturally releasing in our bodies…to wake us up!

Think about times in your very young lives when these feelings and thoughts completely took over your mind: *Are we going to get lost? Are we lost now? Is this going to hurt? Am I going to be OK? Can I do it?* And on and on. These thoughts and feelings serve two really important purposes:

1) They provide opportunities for physical and emotional growth. Maybe you didn't think you were ready, but you were. Maybe you thought you couldn't…and you were right! Maybe you thought, *"I think I can actually do this"* and you did; 2) They provide a drastic contrast to the comfort and complacency (a happiness with what you've already done) of your certainty-filled lives. These thoughts were the fuel of the moment. These uncertainties are what make you who you are.

You might be thinking, *"But Dad, these are the kinds of things that stress me out! I don't want to be lost or hurt!"* Of course you don't. I don't want you to be lost or hurt either. But it's really important to recognize that there are two types of stress: Distress, which is bad stress caused by things that are out of our control, and Eustress, which is caused by the anticipation of the unknown. It's a thrilling exhilaration. It's something you might feel inside right before you take the stage to dance in front of an audience, or before a playoff game, or before you go on a roller coaster.

You know, sometimes I get the most powerful messages from the stupidest places, but this is a good one. I was once, years ago, watching an adult cartoon called *Beavis and Butthead*. Something horrible had happened, and Beavis was really upset. That's when Butthead said, "If nothing ever sucked, how could anything ever be cool?"

If you never struggled to the point of failure, how would you ever feel the joy of achievement? If you never got lost, how could you ever feel the joy of simply being home? If you never felt overwhelming physical pain, how would you appreciate the simple absence of pain? Finally, if you never loved and got your heart broken, how would you ever know the joy of truly being loved?

Think of your certainties, your comforts, as your place to sit and feel the joy of life. But think of your uncertainties as the fuel that joy needs to survive. You really can't have one without the other.

So, as my Aussie friends say, "Give it a go!" Embrace the uncertainties of life; welcome them, as they are just as much a part of a joy-filled life as comfort and certainty. So, chase uncertainties, boys. Then, rest in times of certainty.

I love you boys.

34

Be the Bee

Hey guys! It's Dad.

We've just started a brand-new school year with countless opportunities ahead of each of us. I thought that this would be a perfect time to share a bit of insight that will help keep your academic and social journeys full of smiles.

I heard this idea on a podcast the other night. It came from a guy named John Joseph. You remember John, that Ironman, vegan, punk-rock singer with tons of tattoos? He said, **"Be the Bee, not the Fly."**

At first, I had absolutely no idea what he meant. It didn't get it at all. But when he explained it, it really sunk in.

Let's talk about bees for a second, OK? Typically, the first thing we think about is that bees can sting us, right? But that's only if they need to protect themselves. Bees are actually beautiful and amazing little creatures. They're attracted to flowers and fruits and nuts, and all types of natural beauty. Bees work hard collecting pollen, then they take that pollen and sprinkle it all over the world, helping trees, bushes, and flowers of all kinds to grow and thrive! Did you know that bees pollinate blueberries, apples, melons, almonds and tons of other foods too? They're responsible for the continued growth of the flowers that make our gardens and homes look and smell beautiful…and for the flowers that will make your girlfriends smile and blush too. Without bees…our world would be a dark and dreary place.

Flies, on the other hand, are disgusting, disease-ridden creatures that tear down whatever they touch. They're attracted to garbage, decaying animals, and poop; yes…poop! What's more disgusting than that? They swarm around all this waste, looking for their next meal. Then, before they eat that foul pile of trash and poop…they puke on it! Yep, and then they slurp it right back up. That is not my favorite collection of table manners. Yes, of course, flies play an important role in the circle of life, it's just not a role that I want to be a part of.

So, what do bees and flies have to do with life, or kids in school or just growing up?

Everything!

I want you guys to **Be the Bees** wherever you go. At school and with your friends, be beautiful. Spread smiles and kindness and compliments and empathy wherever you go. I want you to ask questions of your friends, like, "How was summer?" and "How's school going for you so far?" Then I want you to wait. Pause and listen to what they share. And listen to them with the *sole intention* being to understand what they're sharing. Don't spend your attention on what you want to share with them as soon as they stop talking. It's not about "hearing" what they say, but truly listening. Give compliments for the sake of making someone smile, not because you want a compliment in return. Give your energy to consciously and purposefully help others grow into beautiful young people just like you are. Then…they'll become bees too!

Imagine that. A school full of bees, making everything around them look, smell, and feel beautiful. How beautiful would that *bee*?

Be the Bees, boys. Not the flies.

Be the Bees.

I love you guys.

Five Words

Love, Dad.

35

You've Never Made a Wrong Decision

Hey guys! It's Dad.

When I was in college, I had the privilege of taking an economics class taught by Stanford University professor and Austrian economist Kurt Leube. He opened my mind to an amazing truth that took me a long time to really wrap my head around. Sometimes this idea can be the most ridiculous concept to try to grasp. However, when pushed or challenged to take this thought to its end, my beliefs have been wrong—every...single...time—and this simple statement has been right.

We, as human beings, always make the right decision.

Let me write that again.

We **always** make the right decision.

Culturally, personally, privately, we spend so much time beating ourselves up about our life circumstances. Whether it is a career choice, or who we chose as a lover or a spouse, a friend or a business relationship that didn't work out, we're bound to question our past choices. Maybe it was a purchase that we made that later yielded an outcome that was unforeseeable, unintended, and undesired. Maybe we missed out on an investment opportunity that could have changed our lives and the lives of everyone in our family...forever. Our doubts and second guessing have and will continue to go on and on.

When we back up to the point in time when we made these decisions—at that time, with those circumstances, with what knew or thought we knew—the decision was the right one.

It's impossible to put ourselves in that position again because now we are more experienced. We have hindsight. So even if we can bring ourselves to imagine the precise moment when we made that choice—the one that resulted in an outcome other than what we intended or hoped for—we can't do anything about it but dwell on it. We're pretty good at that.

When we're amid the destructive emotions and self-loathing, feelings of hurt and confusion and sorry can be palpable. But we're judging ourselves harshly. We're judging ourselves unfairly, because now we bring with us our new experiences and the ability to see the actual outcome. Now we have the crystal ball.

So when faced with our decision, with the experience we had and the emotion of the moment and the goal we were trying to achieve at the time...we used our faculties to the best of our abilities to give us the best possible outcome. We made the best decision. It was the right decision. Yet we continue to judge ourselves because the outcomes of our decisions were not what we had hoped.

Think about a time when you were charitable or selfless. Maybe you won $10,000 on a TV show and selflessly gave it away to cancer research after losing your mother to cancer. It was kind and charitable. The joy you felt honoring your mother's life and her struggles far outweighed any materialistic possession; any "thing." You made your choice with the understanding that you'd feel better knowing that you made that contribution to such a deserving beneficiary. Later, however, you learn that the organization you donated to was less than forthcoming with where your contribution would go. Then, six months later, you learn that your contribution went to a dishonest non-profit organization whose CEO is sitting on his yacht in the Bahamas, and it's all over the news.

If you're human, you'd likely find yourself swimming in a sea of unhealthy and unhappy emotions like shame, anger, disappointment, sadness, and so on. You'd probably be the subject of your own self-deprecating comments like, "I'm always making stupid choices. I just can't win." But, at the time you chose to make that selfless, well-intentioned charitable contribution...you made the right choice.

Perhaps you went through a bitter divorce. With your unique set of circumstances and with your background and in the mood you were in at the moment the decision was made, you chose to walk away from all of your personal belongings. You just wanted out...NOW. At that time— with the intention of simplifying your new life...or with the intention of causing your spouse inescapable guilt...or proving that you were in control...or any other of a sea of motivations—you chose.

Looking back, you gave up everything. You're now faced with having to rebuild, almost like a college student trying to make ends meet. It's brutal, embarrassing, and exhausting. But...in that moment...hastily or otherwise...you still made that choice—consciously or unconsciously— with the understanding that you would be better off as a result of that decision.

Maybe you robbed a bank. Maybe you were violent toward someone. Maybe you lied and got caught. Maybe you lied and didn't get caught... but you feel horrible. Maybe you climbed Mt. Everest and lost your fingers to frostbite. Maybe you gambled your life savings away. Maybe you even considered ending your life. Those choices, wise or short-sighted, were all made with the belief that you'd be better off on the other side of your choice.

At the end of the day, all too often, we find that the outcome of our decisions is what we struggle with—not the decision itself. "I'm so stupid!" "What was I thinking?" "Why did I do that?" "I can't believe I ended up in this position again!"

There's a hauntingly beautiful song by Joni Mitchell called "Both Sides Now."

I've looked at clouds from both sides now

From up and down and still somehow

It's cloud illusions I recall

I really don't know clouds at all

We can't know the outcomes of our decisions before we make 'em. We can't know what's gonna happen in terms of our careers or our health choices or investments or relationships until they play themselves out. We'll only know if our decisions gave us the result we had anticipated after we've seen both sides.

Perhaps now, from the other side...you will look back at the decisions you've made and afford yourself some well-deserved grace. Now you know that the answer to all those self-sabotaging questions is an easy one.

You made each and every decision you've ever made with the simple and sincere belief that you would be better off on the other side.

36

Seriously, Just SHUT UP!!!

Hey guys! It's Dad.
Seriously! Just writing that title made me feel a little awkward and uneasy.

I'm grateful that it's not often that I hear raised voices in our home. However, it's unlikely that we'll always find ourselves in such a peaceful and respectful environment.

We can't isolate ourselves from the outside world and all of its challenges by hiding out in the comfort of our homes 24/7. We need to live! That means that we need to interact with other people; all kinds of people from all kinds of backgrounds. This subtle change in the way we see things will allow us to focus on how we can be the calm within the storm.

Here's a quick version of a common conversation between my students and me. It happens every term, and often in every class period:

Student: "Mr. B! How come you never raise your voice?"

Me: "Cuz I don't need to."

Student: "But if you don't raise your voice…how do we know that you really, really mean what you're saying?"

Me: "Because I said it."

Back to the offensive title of the post. Why did I use such an ugly and abrasive title? I did it so that we learn to recognize the feelings that this type of interaction can create. Just reading it can change our mood, but being the target of this kind of harsh language can really get to us. It can make us crumble and cower, or we can become aggressive and defensive. It can create fear and anxiety, almost as if we've been startled (like when you're rocking back in a chair and it almost falls over). It can even change the chemistry in our bodies.

There will be times, if there haven't been already, when you'll be confronted by someone who appears to have completely lost their marbles. They might yell and become very animated in their actions and gestures. Their physical appearance may be intimidating as they shake a fist or point a threatening finger. They may curse and scream toward you. I wish I could say that this won't happen…but it does…and it will.

With the certainty of these interactions on our horizon, it's important for us to know how to respond under these circumstances. We need to practice and master exactly how to avoid getting dragged into these types of situations. Beyond that, wouldn't it be fantastic if we could go a step further and learn how to help calm someone or ourselves? These types of situations will collide, uninvited and unwelcomed, into our lives. So, let's get ready to make the best of 'em!

I recently witnessed an upsetting exchange between a man and a woman outside our local grocery store. I think they were married, but it sure wouldn't take many outbursts like the one I saw to send most folks running for the hills…or to a divorce lawyer! The screaming, fist-shaking, and shouting first startled me, then it kinda broke my heart. Why? Because I've been there.

I've handled these types of situations poorly in the past. Not often, but often enough to know that I don't want to be a part of them anymore. (That's how we learn…right?) I know how scary it can be. I know how long the emotions they stir up can last. Although these interactions often last for only an instant, like when someone cuts us off on the highway, they can leave us with unhealthy feelings that can last forever if we let them.

Only after learning how NOT to handle these situations, I learned how to navigate the rough seas of conflict in a way that, at very least, eases discomfort, and at best can turn these experiences into something profoundly positive. I swear, sometimes it feels like magic.

So how do you avoid shouting back when someone gets in your face? What's the right reaction to this type of insult or verbal attack?

Truth? There isn't a "right reaction!" That's the point. Really! A "reaction" is exactly what this type of situation *does not* need. Steven Covey wrote in *The 7 Habits of Highly Effective People* that we need to "create space between stimulus and response." This means that immediately after we feel attacked or disrespected, we need to pause for just split second before we say or do anything.

We need to stop when we first start feeling agitated. Just firmly, consciously push the pause button.

OK! But that's easier said than done!

In the beginning, yes. But, like all healthy behaviors, it becomes more natural (and more rewarding) over time. We can make this a part of our nature; our maturity. We can actually practice not getting angry, not throwing fuel on the fire...not getting "triggered." The split-second immediately after we get triggered, we can simply pause...with absolutely no reaction at all. We don't even have to think yet. Just pause. Practice it! Practice just stopping.

Once we've mastered breaking away from the habit of reacting, then we've matured to the next stage. We can go through the exercises of thinking and visualizing. Think of possible responses *and their likely outcomes*. It's incredible how quickly our brains work during these moments. When we get really good at it, we can think of *and visualize* two or three possible responses *and their outcomes* in a single second!

Imagine the following circumstance:

Johnny throws a water bottle at you.

You pause.

You think, *"Should I throw it back? No. Should I give him the finger and curse at him? No. How about walking over and throwing the bottle in the recycle bin? Maybe! Tell an adult? Sure. Ask him not to throw things? Sure."* Then, after we've thought of an appropriate response...we choose the action that gives US the outcome that WE want. Normally that's a peaceful and positive one.

That pause—that fraction of a second when we don't react but think instead—gives us options. Good options with optimal outcomes. Any of these options can be our response, and any of these responses will lead to a far better outcome than turning around and chucking the bottle at Johnny like we actually wanted to. I promise.

One of the priceless side effects of remaining calm is…Power. People raise their voices when they feel that they're not being heard. The truth is, however, when we raise our voices we aren't actually gaining power or attention. We're losing it. We're losing face. We're losing respect. We're losing credibility and trust. And, although we're desperately trying to capture someone's attention, we're loudly and aggressively demanding their attention…sadly, all we've captured is their fear.

Now that we've raised our voice, our audience is no longer listening to what we're saying. They're either preparing to defend themselves or they're shutting down. They will either meet us at our level of aggression (or even surpass it)…or they'll shut down completely, feeling ashamed, fearful, embarrassed, or resentful. After that, all communication stops. The words may not stop, but they no longer carry any weight or meaning.

After they finally "shut up," they shut down, and that's a pretty hard hit for a relationship to absorb. Whether it's an argument with your brother, your girlfriend, your parents, your friends, or your boss…it's tough to overcome the pain of an angry outburst. Yes, the wounds created by these harsh interactions heal, but they'll always leave a scar. It's best to patiently navigate through and around them.

As you work on mastering the ability to create space between stimulus and response, you'll notice what I see as a self-evident truth playing out. You'll start to see the benefits of responding intelligently as opposed to reacting. You'll start to see that when you respond peacefully and intelligently, you'll no longer go out of your way to avoid what you previously thought might be an uncomfortable situation. You'll be able to talk more openly with people because you know that you won't be drawn into a situation that's now beneath you and behind you.

This skill helps in sport, in class, at work, with family...with everyone. Give it a try. If you fail, try again and again. Just like hitting a curveball...I promise it gets easier with practice.

I love you guys.

Five Words

37

Dad! Do We Have to Go to College?

OK guys, I'm goin' out on a limb here, so bear with me. If I get this one wrong, I'm in trouble!

A few years back I had the privilege of attending a business conference with a guy named Anthony Robbins. He's a pretty neat guy. He makes tons of money coaching people so that they can grow professionally, physically, mentally, and spiritually. He has coached all kinds of people—from a guy who simply wanted to quit smoking, to the world's biggest leaders, the best athletes, the wealthiest business owners, and people who've been through physical and emotional tragedies. So, when he speaks…I listen! I listen very closely.

At this conference I attended, Mr. Robbins was standing in the center of the stage when he gave our group a simple instruction. He said, "If you believe that school is important, raise your hand!"

Of course, every single one of us raised our hands enthusiastically. Then he said something that I'll never forget. He said, in a loud and angry-sounding voice:

"That's complete BULLS@#T! Seriously, you all think that 'Sit down, shut up, and do what I say' is important? It's not and you know it!"

We all sat silently, in shock; almost ashamed. Then he asked:

"Now, how many of you think that education is important?"

It was a huge turning point for me—recognizing the difference between "School" and "Education." Sometimes, simply seeing things from a different point of view can change your lives forever. As for me, I never saw teaching, learning, or education in the same way again.

So how do I see education now? As a teacher who has taught fourth grade through college, it's hard to write this...but the truth is that "school" in and of itself is not important at all.

Yes, "school" teaches us languages and math skills. It may even teach us how to behave in a group. But it misses its target as often as it hits it. More often than that, I think it's aiming at the wrong target.

Consider how time has changed the way we live our daily lives. When I was growing up, your uncle Mark loved a TV show called *Star Trek*. It was a science-fiction show a lot like *Star Wars*. The characters had unimaginable devices like lasers, spaceships, and this really cool "transport" think that would beam you from one place to another...instantly. But one of the coolest things they had was called a "Communicator." It was a hand-held device that was small enough to be carried in a pocket. The user could literally communicate with anyone, anywhere, anytime, right through this little device.

As kids, we talked about how amazing it would be to just be able to reach into your pocket and call anyone in the world...whenever you wanted! That was a world that we couldn't imagine, in our wildest dreams. It was right up there with time travel. But one short generation later, that is exactly the world into which you were born.

While you were reading the paragraph above, I'm sure you were thinking, *"Ummmm...Yeah, Dad! That sounds a lot like our cell phones, but we've got millions of videos, thousands of video games, GPS, access to every movie and every song ever recorded...in fact, every bit of information ever created...at any time...anywhere...and it's all in my pocket."* Yep! We live in an astonishing time.

Now, what does that "one short generation later" have to do with education and the question, "Do we have to go to college?"

Well, just like the Communicator on *Star Trek*, I'd never have dreamed that a kid sitting in his bedroom in Canada could write a song, arrange it, record it, mix it, produce it, create a video for it, publish it... then become a multimillionaire. One short generation ago that literally was as impossible as time travel. Now it happens every day, in every language, all over the world. If someone told me that you can play video games...for a living...and earn enough to own a collection of exotic Italian super-cars, I'd have told them to stay in school! In fact, as a teacher...I probably did! How misguided was that? In fact, now you can make a career about reacting to other people playing video games!!!

Today, you can not only learn to cook by watching YouTube, but you can also use those cooking skills to become an international cooking sensation...on YouTube. You can earn a college degree without even going to "school." Doctors can sit in an office in Dallas and literally do surgery on a patient halfway around the world. There are countless realities that even a decade ago couldn't possibly have been imagined.

"But didn't my schooling help me capitalize on these new technologies?"

Absolutely not! In fact, my formal education may have hurt my chances of success because school taught me…to stay in school!

"Believe me! With no college degree, you'll never succeed…ever."

I heard that from my earliest days.

Today is different, and tomorrow will be too. Today we live in a world that I couldn't imagine when I was your age. With that mindset, doesn't that mean that we don't really have any idea of what's coming in the next 10 to 20 years? How are the world's best public schools supposed to teach us skills, how to use tools, to use languages, technologies, and ideas that don't even exist yet? They can't.

But do they even need to?

This feeling of "not knowing what's coming" might just be what we need to master in order to succeed in our unknowable future. Coming to terms with the simple fact that *we can't know what's coming*…might be most important. If nothing else, that certainty (the certainty that we can't possibly conceive what our lives will be like in 20 years) can empower us! It can give us a new target to hit. One that's not always moving but is all-encompassing.

We know that life won't be the way it is now so we can stop focusing our resources on teaching what's here now. We can start teaching timeless skills and principles such as *critical thinking, cause and effect, and even teaching today's students to be more comfortable being…uncomfortable.* We can teach students how to solve problems without creating bigger ones in the process! We can teach the fact that failing is a function of success, not an obstacle to it, and that the only true failure is giving up.

So how can we be prepared for the unknown? The answer to that question is to focus on three simple things so we can guarantee that we're absolutely ready for whatever's coming next.

1. **Become excellent learners.** Expose yourselves to things that you don't understand, then strive to understand them. This can be sports, the arts, politics, spirituality. Just stay curious and keep learning.

2. **Do what you love.** If you love your work...then it's really not work. For example, I love teaching. So, if I teach during my "work week," then it never really feels like work! Follow your hearts and your passions.

3. **Consider your natural aptitudes.** Keep in mind that you're naturally great at something. That "thing" might be the key to your future successes.

So, should you go to college? I did. I loved it! I learned far more than academics while I was in college. I still believe that, if used properly, college can be priceless. But, if your questions are really, "What should I study?" or "How am I supposed to know what I'm supposed to do when I grow up?" I can simply say:

Keep learning. Be curious. Investigate. See both sides. See all sides! Dig down under the surface of something that doesn't sit right with you. Find out why. Follow joy. Love what you do. Love people.

That is what you do. If you know how to do all of this...and how to be an effective communicator and how to live with proper values, you win. By "win" I don't mean to have the fanciest cars and the biggest houses. I mean "win" in the sense of having the biggest contribution and the most fulfilled hearts, and to love and to feel loved. It's up to you whether college helps you along the way to this ultimate goal.

Live your life the way you choose. It's yours, and it's the only one you get.

One last thing to keep in mind…

If you go back far enough, people believed that if a man traveled faster than a horse he would die. They then believed that if human beings traveled faster than one mile per minute they would die. Then, science passionately proclaimed that man cannot survive breaking the sound barrier. Now, despite all of those ridiculous "scientifically backed" and disproved assumptions, scientists claim that traveling at the speed of light is impossible. What do you think?

We—your parents, your teachers, your government—are clueless, and I'm OK with that. That's the way it's meant to be. But when I'm long gone, when you guys have those new pocket time machines, will you set the time for today and come back so I can give you guys just one more hug?

I love you, boys.

#5words

Love, Dad.

38

Perspective Changes Everything

Hey guys. It's Dad!
I wanted to share a couple of stories that have truly helped me during times when I have struggled to "keep calm" and behave in a healthy, positive, supportive way. People lie. People have accidents. People make mistakes. We all make mistakes.

There are two ideas or strategies that I have relied on that have sincerely helped me. I learned them from stories that I heard from an author who recently passed way. It's a shame that he's gone, but what he taught me, through his writing, is always with me. In fact, it's always with you.

Here's the first story. While you read it, imagine how your emotions come into play. Notice how your feelings change at the end of the story.

A battleship was on an exercise at sea, and in very bad weather. The captain was on the bridge, where he controls the ship. It was very foggy and the seas were rough. Just after dark, the look-out told the captain that he spotted a light on the starboard side. The captain quickly asked if the light was steady or moving. The look-out told him that the light was steady, meaning they were on direct collision course with that ship!

The captain ordered the ship's look-out to send out a message, "Change course 20 degrees. We are on collision course."

A message came back, "Advisable for you to change course."

The captain messaged again, "I am a captain! Change your course 20 degrees."

A reply came back, "I am a seaman second class. You had better change course 20 degrees."

The captain was furious now. He sent back an angry message, "I AM A BATTLESHIP! CHANGE COURSE IMMEDIATELY!"

Back came a simple message saying, "I am a lighthouse."

I bet that the captain probably felt like a complete jerk! From calm, to furious, to embarrassed. That's a huge range of emotions that never needed to happen. If he knew that the other person wasn't challenging him but helping him, he'd never have been upset. If he knew that the other person was sending those messages to save his crew, and to save his ship from crashing into the rocks during that stormy night, he would have felt grateful, not angry.

But what if we don't know why? How should we behave? Wasn't the captain right to send his messages?

This second story helps us to understand how important it is not to make judgments, but to always behave with compassion and understanding. This story really affected me in a powerful and positive way. This is the story that taught me to live our little family's mission: "Always be a gentleman." This is a true story of an experience that the author I wrote about earlier lived through.

One morning in New York, people were sitting quietly on a subway train. Some were reading newspapers, some were lost in thought, some were resting with their eyes closed. It was a calm, peaceful morning.

Then, suddenly, a man and his children entered the subway car. The children were so loud and disrespectful that instantly the peaceful morning was interrupted.

The man sat down next to me and closed his eyes, apparently not caring about how crazy his kids were behaving. The children were yelling and screaming. They were throwing things, and falling down, even grabbing people's newspapers out of their hands. They were SO rude, but their dad still didn't do anything. He just sat there, zoned out.

It was difficult not to feel irritated. I could not believe that he could just let his kids run wild like that and do nothing about it, taking no responsibility at all for their behavior.

It was easy to see that it wasn't just me who was aggravated. Everybody on the train was getting aggravated too. So, after being patient for such a long time, I finally turned to the man and sternly said, "Excuse me! Sir! Your children are really disturbing a lot of people. Will you please control them a little better?"

The man looked like he had just woken up from a deep sleep, not knowing what was going on around him. Then he softly said something that I'll never forget.

"Oh wow. You're so right. I'm terribly sorry. I guess I should do something about it. We just came from the hospital where their mother passed away about an hour ago. I don't really know what to do or think, and I guess they don't know how to handle it either. I'm sorry."

Imagine that! What did you feel when you read that the poor man had just lost his wife; the mother of his children? He wasn't in fact irresponsible and rude. He was lost in his heart and in his head. Did your emotions change as soon as you learned the truth? Did your feelings of anger and resentment toward him go away, only to be replaced with feelings of compassion and helplessness? Didn't you want to comfort him, rather than scold him?

Did everything change in an instant? It's fascinating, really. After reading both stories, the only thing that changed in an instant was our emotions. The lighthouse was still a lighthouse, and the poor man's wife had really passed away. Absolutely nothing had changed, yet everything had changed. We learned why. We learned why the ship captain and the man on the train behaved the way that they did. The only thing that changed was in our understanding.

It's amazing how as soon as we know the whole truth our emotions, our anger, our sadness, our resentment all wash away in an instant. So why don't we just live like that? Well, we can. I do! Or at least I try.

It's always easier to accept that we don't know why people behave the way that they do. It's not just easier on us…but it leads to a much, much more peaceful life.

Why is that man driving like an idiot? What a jerk! Well, maybe his baby is horribly sick and he's rushing her to the hospital. Or…maybe he's an idiot! *Why is that boy in my class always sleeping instead of doing his work?* Well, maybe he stayed up all night playing video games. Or…maybe he stayed up all night listening to his mom and dad fighting. Maybe nobody was there to comfort him and make him feel safe. Maybe, just maybe, this classroom is the only place where he feels safe.

Ultimately, we shouldn't change our behaviors based on other peoples' attitudes and behaviors. We should simply behave as gentlemen do. That will always work. Always.

That doesn't mean that you can't get upset, or you don't have the right to feel angry or disappointment or hurt by someone. Those are natural feelings, and a normal part of a healthy life. But if taking a moment to wonder "why" can help alleviate some of those feelings, then it was worth it to jot down these two little stories.

With practice, it becomes easier to simply say to yourself, "I just don't know why he is a bully or why she stole something or why they got into a fight, so I will behave with compassion and caring, rather than anger and resentment."

It does get easier too, the more you practice it. I promise.

Oh. That man! The one who told the stories. His name is Stephen Covey. His books have helped me a lot. We can read 'em together if you want. They're amazing.

I love you boys.

Love, Dad.

39

Learning to Let Go

Hey guys! It's Dad.

Today, although our home was empty, my head sure wasn't. I was cleaning up the house after an often-frantic weekday morning when I realized that I couldn't seem to find peace in my head. I couldn't seem to stop the constant thinking. I wanted to be "Present," in the moment, but I kept thinking about choices I'd made, and if those choices were the best choices I could make. I just kept creating this stress and noise in my mind about thoughts and things of yesterday. Then it hit me. I remembered a story that I'd heard years and years ago called "Two Monks and a Maiden."

One day, hundreds of years ago, two monks were traveling through the forests and valleys of rural China, on a journey to a distant Buddhist temple on a mountaintop. These two monks had made a promise to Buddha (their god) to focus only on their spiritual growth, and not to be distracted by the desires of modern comforts, beautiful women, and other worldly things. In fact, they had taken an oath to not speak with, touch, or even look at women. They were to keep their focus at all times.

One monk was old and very wise. The other was young, enthusiastic, and eager to show the older, wiser monk how properly he could behave. This walk would take them several hours to complete, all spent in silence, thinking about the sights and sounds of their journey, and thinking about their faith; their spiritual growth.

After a couple hours of silently hiking through the trails and villages, the two monks approached a small creek that, after days of heavy rains, had turned into a raging river. As they approached the river, they noticed a young woman on the side of the river. She needed to pass, but couldn't possibly survive had she tried to cross the rushing river.

Without a moment's hesitation, the tiny old monk offered his help. The young woman accepted his help, and the old monk lifted her with all of his might to carry her across the river. The young monk was in shock. He couldn't understand how the older, wiser monk could break his vow; his promise.

Several moments later, the old monk set the young woman safely on the bank on the other side of the river. As the young monk awaited his return, he could barely contain his aggravation, frustration, and disappointment. Soon, the wise old monk climbed from the river, and continued his silent journey toward the old temple in the mountains.

One hour passed, then another, and another. The entire time, the young monk's blood was pumping in anger and confusion. After yet another hour of hiking in silence, the young monk couldn't keep it in any longer. He blurted out, "I can't believe that you did that! We're not even allowed to gaze upon a young woman, yet you walked over and picked her up and carried her! How can you justify this behavior?" The wise old monk didn't miss a stride when he said,

"I set down that fair maiden nearly four hours ago. Are you still carrying her?"

The two monks walked, silently, side by side, into the temple. The wise old monk, walking in peace; the young monk deep in thought about the lesson that he'd learned on his journey.

Sometimes we can lose the beautiful moments that we're living in by allowing the fears, disappointments, and regrets of our pasts to steal them away. Be aware of this. Be in the moment. Allow the very moment that you're in to be experienced as it is. Allow it to be cherished, enjoyed, and protected from the fears, disappointments, and regrets of our past.

There's another lesson buried in that story too. It is to understand that the laws and rules of our society, our schools, our homes, are there for a reason. These laws and rules protect us. However, there are going to be moments in your life when you have to trust yourself to do the right thing in the right moment, even if it's against the laws or rules of your surroundings.

You are bright young men. You are gentlemen. You may be faced with a situation like the wise old monk, where you feel compelled to do something that is against the rules, but for the right reason. I trust you to do the right thing, because the right thing is guiding you each day.

Let go of yesterday. It no longer exists, so don't carry its burdens. Trust in yourself to recognize when doing the right thing and doing what you're told are different. Then, be confident in your decision, and let it go.

Be in this moment. This moment is all that we will ever have.

Remember the joy that being a gentleman brings.

I love you boys.

Love, Dad.

40

It's Time to Stop Celebrating
Our Independence

Here's an uncomfortable look at the celebration of our nation's independence—fireworks, BBQs and all.

As I grow, my thoughts and beliefs periodically waver as I'm exposed to new information and consider alternate perspectives to my own. I think that's probably pretty normal. We live. We learn. We grow. At least that's how it's supposed to be.

My thoughts on this evolving nation and my feelings about our yearly celebration of our nation's independence seem to be stuck, and they go something like this:

Each year my ponderings of the 4th of July start over again. Traditionally, the celebrations of the Fourth typically consist of a gathering of our closest friends and family, good food, sunshine, swimming, and BBQ, all capped off with watching fireworks! These are all things that I treasure. Our forefathers (and foremothers) had unimaginable courage and dreams that are clearly worth celebrating. There's something heart-warming and memorable about these get-togethers.

That said, especially when it comes to traditions, the "Why do we do this?" always undermines my mental monologue. So, other than for the fun of it, what's it all really about, and how is this "independence" thing working out for us anyway?

We all start our lives completely dependent. Our nation started like that too. However, as human beings, we learn and grow—eventually reaching physical, financial, mental, and emotional independence. We can do things on our own. We no longer need the support of our parents and caregivers in order to survive. Ignoring the arbitrary age of 18 which signifies "adulthood" in the US, people typically become independent sometime between the ages of 16 and 22. The US became independent on July 4th, 1776. Happy Birthday!

Each year, on the Fourth, we raise our flags in our yards; we wear our red, white, and blue; and we carry on with our celebrations. But year after year I keep wondering, isn't there another step to our evolution? Individually, isn't independence just another step on our path to interdependence—working together? Don't we need each other in order to truly thrive? Aren't we, as a society, as a nation, "better together"?

If dependency comes first, and independence second, doesn't interdependence come next? We're born dependent, work hard to become independent, then bring our strengths and wisdom together, and truly work together to achieve unimaginable goals. Aren't our ultimate individual and collective utilities optimized when we work together?

I'd love to see the US start to show more maturity, more wisdom, more social development, and more interdependence. I'm starting to see glimpses of a shift in mindset from the younger generations. I'm grateful for that. Maybe from the shadows will come true interdependence, and with that…peace.

As Lennon said, "Imagine…"

Let's keep celebrating our Independence on the 4th of July…but let's continue growing too. Let's celebrate this incredible, empowering, world-changing milestone as another step toward peace. But we can't rest on our laurels. There's no need (and with today's circumstances, no time) to stop and rest. We've still got work to do.

Today, from the bottom of my heart, I wish you ALL a happy Independence Day. It is with the hope that the coming years add another holiday to the calendar…with more swimming, more sunshine, more BBQ, more baseball, and maybe we'll hold off on the fireworks. Maybe we'll call that day…"Interdependence Day." And hey…let's make that holiday last a week.

"I hope some day you'll join us, and the world will be as one."

41

The Crescendo of Life

I sit, writing this post, amidst a sea of emotion.

Around the time of writing this, the world lost a world-class musician and songwriter to suicide, we lost a world-class motorcycle racer to a senseless bicycle accident, and we lost 22 unwitting and undeserving fans at an Ariana Grande concert in Manchester to terrorism.

Yes, I feel anger, confusion, sadness, and disbelief. But, rather than sitting mired in the emotion and the gravity of circumstances, I wanted to see if I could make sense of it—or better, make use of it—so here it goes.

I don't take lightly the losses that we've sustained, nor the devastating sorrow that the families of those who've passed must be feeling. There are no adequate words to express my sorrow and sadness. But the follow things I understand to be true.

- Chris Cornell, of Soundgarden and Temple of the Dog, had struggled with depression and addiction. As devastating as it is, Chris' is not an isolated or even an uncommon event.

- Nick Hayden was involved in a cycling accident. Although he frequently raced motorcycles at speeds well in excess of 200mph, this wasn't what brought the premature end to his life. While training, for fitness purposes, he was senselessly and fatally hit by a car on his bicycle. As I know all too well, this is also not an isolated or uncommon event.

- The men, women, and children killed in the Manchester bombing were simply celebrating life. In a vulnerable position, with their guards down, they were attacked in the most cowardly way. These types of attacks too are no longer isolated nor uncommon. They will continue, and will likely increase in frequency and severity, until the entire world appreciates and adopts the highest level of social development: interdependence.

As Americans, we pride ourselves on our independence. But to what end? We've got to look beyond the egoistic point of independence, and finally graduate to a position of true interdependence—one of relying on each other rather than fighting with or exploiting each other.

With all of that said, with a sincere effort to make sense through the sadness, I'm left with this almost rhetorical question, "So what now?"

Initially, this may appear off the point, but I promise…I'll bring it back around.

Both through watching TED talks, as well as listening to the Tim Ferriss podcast, I've been exposed to an organization called "The Zen Hospice Project" in San Francisco. Their mission is as follows:

"Our mission is to help change the experience of dying and caregiving. We create space for living that offers the opportunity for individuals, their loved ones and caregivers to find comfort, connection, and healing in this shared human experience. Through our pioneering model of care, we inspire each other to live fully."

The cases and stories that I've followed are as diverse as they are inspiring, from its founder's life-changing (in fact, world-changing) experience of simply holding a melting snowball, to an ALS patient deciding to start smoking, to a terminal cancer patient's stoic "Bucket List" trip down the Colorado River. The spirit of these stories, of these people, are stern reminders that if we live with the fear of death we are robbing ourselves of living our full lives.

It's not about the formal tending of a diseased body, but what I see as a ringing in or a celebration of the end of one's time on earth. Not in a sterile room full of latex gloves and beeping machines, but surrounded by loved ones and life and dreams and comfort and support. To paraphrase Zen Hospice Project's founder, BJ Miller, "Ending with a Crescendo of Life"

If I may, let me ask these questions:

What if you were told that you had only two weeks to live? Really! What would you do? Don't read on. Just stop and think about what you would do; about what matters; about who matters. What would Chris Cornell, or Nicky Hayden, or the sea of victims in Manchester do if they knew the end was so near?

What if you only had a day left to live? That's all! If you were told that by this time tomorrow it would all end, what would you do? What matters to you, sincerely? Who would you spend that day with?

Now, finally, pushing that question to an absurd but effective end... what would you do if you only had now? What if this very moment was the last moment that you had? What matters to you now? WHO matters to you now?

We don't often think of this, nor act on it, but, in fact, this is the case. This our only moment. This "now" is all we have.

Are you going to wait until you're gone before you start truly living? Equally as compelling—and something I've seen too often—are you going to wait for the next funeral service to stand up and share what you really feel about your spouse, your brother, your friend, your father? We can't know when the end will come, but we have *now*. Tell 'em now.

We all know that we cannot quit our jobs and run off to the ocean with our loved ones to spend some long overdue time together. No, I don't encourage irresponsibility. I will, however, beg you not to trade away a single moment more than you absolutely have to.

Are you really going to trade life's most important moments, our only moments, in order to buy another handbag, or another pair of shoes, or so you can upgrade your 55" TV for an 85" model? Watching *The Voice* on a bigger TV can't possibly be as enriching or fulfilling as working on that book you always wanted to write, or traveling to see an old friend, or tutoring a kid on his math homework, or learning how to surf, or taking a walk with your spouse, or listening to a wise old woman share what life's really about.

Not long ago, I worked with a gentleman who was at the end of his professional career. He worked in real estate but he always wanted to become a pastor. The time just never seemed right. At 60 years of age, he gave serious consideration to going back to school for four full years in an effort to pursue his dreams. He hesitated, postponed, and procrastinated, which ultimately lead to this brief but powerful conversation with a close friend and mentor.

My former colleague: "I haven't registered for school yet. I just can't bring myself to do it. It just seems unrealistic, maybe even irresponsible. Think about it. I'm going to be 64 years old when I'm done with my four-year program."

His mentor: "How old will you be in four years if you don't go to school?"

Again, sitting here sincerely heartbroken for the families who've lost their loved ones, I implore you to live...to be your absolute best. Look inside at what truly make you shine, then go do that. You will become the richest "you" possible; and those you love, those around you, will reap the rewards of your journey.

I love you guys.

Five Words.

42

Don't Wait for Your Golden Years— These Are the Golden Years!

Hey guys! It's Dad.

It's funny when, where, and how we learn our life lessons. If we're plugged in, they seem to be around every corner. This one was no exception.

Last night I had a really peaceful dream; a dream that taught me something and it made me smile. In my dream, a father was speaking with his young son. I don't think it was me in the dream, but I could feel how much the father loved his son. He wanted nothing more than to help his son achieve happiness and success in his life. Their conversation went something like this:

Father: "Hey buddy! So, what do you think you'd like to do when you're older? You know, for a job? What interests you? Remember, if you love what you do, you'll never mind having to wake up early to go to work!"

Son: "I want to fly, Dad!"

Father (with a chuckle): "Don't we all, my man!"

Son: "I mean, I guess I really do like playing video games. I love basketball too. It's awesome! I kinda like art, like painting and stuff. But (laughing) I really wanna fly! Not like an airplane, but just me... flying."

Father: "Well those are all great interests. Are those things that you'd like to pursue now, or in the near future? Did you want me to sign you up for some art classes, or to a basketball rec league?"

Son: "Uhhh...No thanks, Dad. I just want to go watch TV."

Father: "Well, if you want to succeed, if you want to really create a comfortable and happy future for yourself, we might want to look into it sooner rather than later. I can set it up for you. You just let me know. OK?"

After a long pause:

Father: "Think about it, kiddo. Do you want to be a big fish in a small pond, or do you want to be a big fish in the ocean? The earlier you start, the more experience you'll have with whatever you're doing. Don't you want to be the big fish?"

Son: "I'm not a fish, Dad. I'm a bird. I want to fly. I really just want to fly."

The dad smiled and hugged his son tightly and told him, "Then you go fly, little man! You go fly!"

That's it! It was pretty awesome. I woke up in one of those "aha" moments. It reminded me of how important it is to be ourselves! We don't have to strive for the "American Dream." We can make our own dreams. You could live in a bus at the beach and surf all year. Heck, you could video yourself doing it and probably make a killing; a happy, peaceful living. And the whole time, you'd be surrounded by people who share your passion. You could open a nursery and teach people how to grow and cook their own food. You could work for the president, and maybe knock some sense into him or her.

Just keep your spirit plugged in all the time. Make sure that the path you're taking leads to peace and happiness within yourself. Make sure that you let yourself fly!

My generation is the end of an era that taught us to "Do well in school, go to college, get married, buy a house, have kids, then retire and enjoy your golden years." By "golden years" they mean "when you're really old."

It's sad to say, but sometimes *those* golden years never come. But…I promise that the very best years will never come if you keep looking into the future to find them.

The golden years are here right now! Enjoy your lives right now. Explore your interests now. Of course, those interests will probably change; and if they do, explore new ones.

If you're a fish, I hope you swim in the ocean. And if you're a bird, I hope you fly to wherever your dreams lead you.

I love you guys.

#5words

Dad

43

I Just Want to Get Away from It All

Have you ever worked on a maze? You know, the little puzzles where you have to navigate from the start to the end through a series of "forks in the road." On a few occasions I've had to start at the end of the maze, then work backward to find my way to the start. These thoughts, this post, came together sort of like that. So here it is…sort of backward.

According to the Outdoor Industry Association's Outdoor Recreation Economy Report, we spend an estimated $650 billion each year on outdoor recreation: camping, hunting, fishing, hiking, etc. The way I see it, it's the amount of money we spend to escape.

No phones.

No TVs.

No computers.

Just "getting away from it all."

Think about that number again: $650 billion. I know that each night on TV we hear newscasters throwing around the words "billion" and "trillion" like it's loose change that we found in the cushion of our sofa.

But $650 billion is a ton of money. To be more accurate, at one gram per $100 bill, it's 7,100 tons of money. Visualize stacks of $100 bills. If you were to stack up $650 billion in $100 bills, the stack would reach the very tip of the spire on the top of the Empire State Building…1,584 times…every year.

So what! So we like to camp and hunt and fish! What about it?

Yes, clearly we do; myself included. But while I was thinking about that tendency I found myself thinking, *"Why do we spend that much money…getting away from the lives that we've worked our entire lives to create?"*

To add insult to injury, that report doesn't include our vacations! It's not that trip to Hawaii, or to Disney World. It's only the "Let's just pack the tent, the ice-chest, the Coleman stove, and head off for a few days" kinds of getaways.

But sincerely, doesn't it sound nice: to just get away from it all, even just for a single night? Sadly, hasn't that idea almost become cliche? I've said it myself, countless times. "Man! It's gonna be so nice to just get away for a few days; to reconnect with the family; to find some peace."

But get away from what? What is so bad in our day-to-day lives that we forsake the current moments in anticipation of getting away from it? So now I find myself questioning the entire idea. Not the getting away part; I question the lifestyles that we've worked so painstakingly to create.

Don't get me wrong. I love the creature comforts of suburban America. I really do. A hot bath, the sofa with a blanket and the remote. It's so nice, but at what cost?

If you live in the US, most of us spend, at an absolute minimum, 13 years (K-12) of our lives in school. For many of us, it's 17 years; K-12, plus college. For a few more, it goes far, far beyond that, into multiple years of graduate and post-graduate work. All of this cost, energy, and effort with the sole intention of achieving that "American Dream."

We earn that dream job, doing something we love. We get married, then we buy a house and a car. Then we're off to the races! And we, as a society, do that specifically because…um…'cuz…well, because that's what we do.

We, seemingly unconsciously but incessantly, update and upgrade and replace what we already have. We buy bigger TVs, new kitchen cabinets, a bigger car, a smaller car, or maybe a money-saving electric car. If we're really "succeeding," we almost immediately start planning a vacation; our next get-away.

We've just started our lives and families and we already need to get away from it all. Yeah. We need to get away from that new TV, the new kitchen cabinets, and even that German car in the driveway with the "new-car smell."

In the book *A New Earth*, Eckhart Tolle writes, "The ego wants to want more than it wants to have." This is an incredibly uncomfortable truth illustrating the fact that the rush of joy that we feel when we buy a new TV or a new car or even new shoes is fleeting and temporary. However, the pressure and the obligation to pay for is not so temporary.

Too many times I've watched vibrant, passionate, loving, and hard-working young people, wishing their weeks and months away in hopes that their obligatory two weeks off per year correspond with the two weeks that their spouses get off. Oh…and I hope the kids will be out of school at that time too.

Have we, in spite of massive and concerted efforts, taken the wrong path? Are we stuck in some sort of developmental and karmic loop? Is it "Monkey See. Monkey Do"? Are we doing what we do because it's what we see?

I don't think so. I, with all of who I am, believe that we do all of it, tirelessly and thanklessly, because we've not been taught that there's another way.

Stephen R. Covey, the author of *The 7 Habits of Highly Effective People*, wrote, "If the ladder is not leaning against the right wall, then every step we take just gets us to the wrong place...faster."

From my viewpoint, where many of us find ourselves, individually and collectively, can't be as fantastic as we were promised. If it is, why do we daydream about (and spend billions of dollars each year) leaving it?

I think that's it. That's the question that I'm struggling with. Have we become incredibly efficient at accumulating stuff? Have we, albeit unwittingly, completely lost our focus on what actually matters? Are we allowing—in fact, encouraging—the simplest of joys to elude us while we work our backsides off in pursuit of temporarily satisfying our ego's insatiable appetite? Have we been brainwashed by marketing moguls? Are we that sheepish? That naive?

Yes. In the meantime, we repeatedly put a tiny fraction of what we've worked so hard to accumulate into a suitcase, only packing what we need, then pay thousands or tens of thousands of dollars to leave everything else behind.

Me? For 45 years, I was guilty as charged. Now I'm trying to break that cycle; at least in my little family of three. I want to be outside. I want to see the world. I want to leave it all behind. In fact, I want to leave it all on the shelves at the big box stores. Is a more minimal lifestyle in my family's near future? It sure feels like it...and that feels right.

Hugs.

44

What's on the Other Side of Chance?

"A ship is safe in harbor, but that's not what ships are for."
– William G. T. Sheed

Hey guys. It's Dad.

I want to encourage you, and nurture in you, a willingness to take chances. I know that it sounds obvious enough, but sometimes taking chances can be scary. In fact, it's pretty much always scary, even for me. Amazing things happen when we take chances. Life changing, world-changing things happen when we are brave enough to take chances. Truthfully, they only happen when we take chances.

Years ago, I managed a night-club in the Bay Area. I can't tell you how many hours I spent listening to people pour their hearts out about their current life circumstances. Their thoughts and spirits were buried in fear. They seemed almost paralyzed by it, unwilling to take necessary action to change their lives. They'd often ask me about relationships and careers, adventures and sports, travel and hobbies. It wasn't long before I realized that my responses, my direction and encouragement, always seemed to take the same point of view. I could sum it up by simply saying, "Take a chance and see!"

My side of these conversations often sounded something like this:

Imagine yourself on the top of a steep, steep mountain bike trail, or maybe a ski slope. It's so steep that it looks impossible to go down. You're all geared up, clipped in, ready to go, but you're absolutely freaked out about how badly this might turn out. Now…how are you going to handle it? What are you going to do?

Well, here are your choices:

A) You can go down very cautiously, with the brakes on, slowly inching your way down, laboring to making sure that you don't fall…or…B) you can release the brakes, choose the best path that you can see, and let it rip!

The likely outcomes of these two strategies could not be more different from each other.

If you take the cautious and methodical approach, there's really only one probable outcome: You're gonna make it down. You'll have white knuckles, your heart will be beating like crazy, you'll be gasping for air, and ultimately it's over. But hey…you'll be safe. When you're done with this approach your life will be the exactly the same as it was before; exactly as it was at the top of the mountain…but now you're at the bottom.

So what changes if you risk it; if you take a chance and just go for it?

This gives you two very different possibilities:

1) You go for it. You go bombing down the mountain, almost completely out of control. Then it happens. You have an absolutely horrible wipe-out; bouncing off the ground like a ragdoll wishing that Red Bull really did give you wings. Your bike and gear are strewn all over the mountainside. My buddies and I gave this less than desirable outcome a loving nickname. We call it "A Yard Sale!" Gloves are over here! A boot is over there! Goggles? Has anybody seen my goggles? As you continue your tumble, you let out an uncontrolled howl that's usually accompanied by a trip to the emergency room for some stitches and an X-ray or two. Take it from me—these wipe-outs can, and usually do, have a massive impact on your life. Still, I wouldn't trade 'em for the world. My friends, my family, and I still laugh about these experiences today, commenting…"Well, it seemed like a good idea at the time!"

2) The other possible outcome is that you actually make it down in one piece! You lean over the edge. All you see is that the ground disappears below you, then reappears just before the bottom. The middle of the run isn't even visible to you until you drop in. So, you let off the brakes and let it roll! With acceleration unlike anything you've ever felt, you go flying down the mountain. You're dodging rocks and trees, grunting and groaning as instincts of self-preservation take over, jumping over stumps and boulders like some X-Games athlete. You see your life pass before your eyes about a million times. Then…right before the mountain flattens out at the bottom, you let out an uncontrolled howl that's usually accompanied by the biggest grin you've ever had in your life.

Just like the cautious approach, you've got white knuckles and your heart is beating like crazy, and you're at the bottom. But this time you did it. You took a massive chance, and you'll never be the same for it!

You may never do it again...or you may catch your breath, laugh with your buddies, and climb right back to the summit to have another go! Either way, I can promise you one thing. Whether you wiped out or you made it...your life will never be the same. It will never be the same because you took the chance.

Keep taking chances. Don't be afraid to fail. Failure is a function of success. Don't think that you can't do it. You can! Think about this... Noah built the ark. Do you think he was nervous? "Wait...God. You want me to do WHAT?" But the very finest engineers and craftsmen in the world built the *Titanic*, and we all know how that worked out.

Sometimes we succeed, and sometimes we learn. So think about what could happen if you succeed. Consider what could happen if you fail. Then think about how your spirit feels if you don't even try.

So what's on the other side of chance? It's life; real, rich life.

"Should I accept that job in Rhode Island?"

I don't know. Would you be happier if you got the job?

"Should I climb Mt. Everest?"

I don't know. Is that a dream of yours? If so, why have you waited this long? Let's pack!

"Should I ask that pretty girl to the dance?"

Yes! Definitely yes.

I love you, boys. I hope that you live your lives, rather than just survive them.

Take chances. I promise. I'll be here to pick you up if you fall…

OK…*when* you fall.

I love you boys.

Five Words.

Love, Dad.

45

When Did We Lose Our Way?

If you're at all like me, you're busy. You're too busy. You're insanely busy, and it's not just your schedule! The sad fact is that even when our schedule is clear, our minds are cluttered. We have become overstimulated and overwhelmed. Our attention has been hijacked and our minds are littered with the chaos of our days; the chaos that we unwittingly invited into our lives. But don't fret, we're a very adaptable species. We can handle it! In fact, we're so adaptive that regardless of the avalanche of activities crowding the space from our calendars (and those of our kids) we press on! Our efficiencies soon create more space to fill, and busy becomes very busy, and finally completely dysfunctional.

We've come to a point where we actually no longer think. Contemplate that for a moment. We no longer actually think. Thinking just happens, and it happens incessantly. I'm not talking about the thinking that actually serves us. I'm talking about the nonstop thinking that happens between what's serving us. Are we really in control of it? Are we in control of any of it? Then, when it's no longer possible to grind through the hours and days filled with hyper-productivity and hyper-stimulation, we find ourselves daydreaming about better days.

"If I could only…"

"Wouldn't it be amazing if…"

"I can't wait until…"

We force our minds into thoughts of times, people, and places other than here…now.

"Wait a minute. Don't tell me I don't think! Of course, I think. I'm thinking right now!" See…I thought you might be a little like me. OK, clearly we contemplate. We ponder. We're creative, and in a crisis, we're focused and attentive. But can we at least agree that there's definitely a lot of idle noise going on upstairs?

Our thinking helps us to solve problems! In fact, we love solving problems. We love it so much that there's a thriving, multi-billion-dollar industry whose sole purpose is to create problems for it! Riddles, puzzles, crosswords, and on and on, keep our minds busy when our minds aren't busy being productive. It's calming to draw or color, or to do a crossword or build puzzles. But why? Why is struggling through a 1,000-piece puzzle of the sky so relaxing? Because it makes us focus! We're good at that kind of thinking. It's the times when we're not focused that our minds completely melt down and run away from us…and that's *no bueno*.

We've lost our individual and collective abilities to simply "be." We just "do." We're no longer "human beings." We've become "human doings."

There are tools and strategies—both new and old—designed to calm our obsessing minds, to encourage us to be mindful, to be present. Meditation, yoga, even rigorous exercise can wipe away the noise. And when all of that noise is gone…we're left with space. This can be a horrifying prospect for some, but when used effectively that space can save our health, our relationships…and maybe even our sanity!

So it's possible to create healthy habits of using our minds to think for us rather than continuing to allow our minds to use us so they can think. BUT WE DON'T.

Why don't we use these thousand-plus-year-old techniques to calm our minds? Why do we resort to mind-numbing medications and other vices to calm and quiet our minds?

We have become masters of efficiency instead of effectiveness. We have calendars, alarms, and notifications telling us where to be and when. We no longer watch what's on TV. We watch what we recorded on the DVR because we're too busy to watch when the shows air. Then, with the expertise of a surgeon, and a death grip on our remote, we fast-for-ward through the commercials, even skipping over the "boring" parts. It's almost like a race to the end. "I really just want to see who got voted off anyway." We binge-watch. We buy take-out or fast-food, or even faster still, we microwave our dinners at home. To quote one of my favorite '80s bands, The Fixx, "I'm cooking with microwaves, to warm up food that's not seen the soil."

Sadly though, through all of our recently adopted abilities to multi-task and execute our schedules, we still, somehow, can't find a way to get to sleep on time. Then, once we're finally in bed, we're so wound up from the pace of the day, and plagued by anxiety and anticipation of the days to come, that we can't get to sleep—"I just can't stop thinking!" Then... DING! We're up at dawn with a cup of coffee that's big enough to keep the Tabernacle Choir awake for a week. We eat our breakfast in the car right after we finish our makeup, and all of this somehow comes together betwixt and between a flurry of tweets, posts, and text messages. Then somehow, with virtually no time left on the clock, we justify our chaotic lives either by claiming that it makes us happy, or more naively with the belief that it might make us happy at some time in the future.

In short, we do all of this with the goal of being happy. In the end, we really just want to feel joy.

We daydream in vain. *"I wonder what my life would be like if things were different."* Well, the simple act of wondering is like speaking in your mind where nobody's there to listen, not even you. Or it's like scurrying around, trapped in a cage, looking for answers, looking for an exit, only to learn that the cage is locked within your head.

But, if we take the power back—if we spend a few moments each day actually wondering, thinking on our own, using our minds as they were intended—we just might break that cycle. The conscious act of purposefully wondering, when the process is unencumbered by fear, naturally leads us to only one place—a place of joy.

"How so?"

I thought you'd never ask.

To find that moment, that peacefulness, that joy that really might be our end goal, takes a journey. It's not going to find you. You actually need to get up, get moving, and find it. Finding that happiness, that joy, takes exploration. It takes action. It takes risk. We might have to face our fears. We might fail. We might lose our way. We might walk through the valley of the shadow of death, and we might get hurt. But we'll be alive!

"I wonder what's around the next corner!"

"I wonder what she's going to say!"

"I wonder why I'm so apathetic!"

"I wonder if I could ever…"

And that's how it starts. Notice that those 'wonder' statements above aren't actually even questions. They are statements! They describe your action. That action will bring life to your journey.

Wondering—that conscious curiosity—leads to exploration (both self-exploration, and physical exploration). In turn, when it's not stifled by fear, exploration leads to discovery. Discovery then leads to truths, which, when bravely faced, lead to acceptance of such truths. That acceptance of what truly is, the now—THAT is enlightenment. Enlightenment is the most direct path to joy. In fact, it is joy.

Of course, there are a number of important emotional and physical pieces to the puzzle, but acceptance of the truth is right there at the top. In the words of Viktor Frankl from his 1946 book, *Man's Search for Meaning*, "Everything can be taken from a man but one thing: the last of the human freedoms—to choose one's attitude in any given set of circumstances, to choose one's own way." So hold onto that thought as you start your journey. If you're doing it right, your journey will bring struggles. But through those struggles, you don't need to wear a grimace. They can just as easily bring a smile. So don't fear these struggles. Embrace them. Dance with your fears.

We are often slowed, or even stopped, by our fears. "I wonder what it would be like to…" "I wonder if I could…" "But if I quit my job…" and so on. Of course, I don't advocate carelessness, but perhaps fearlessness. Push yourself for yourself. Get out of your comfort zone. Perhaps nothing sums it up better than this simple quote by author Suzy Kassem: "Fear kills more dreams than failure ever will."

Joy. It's such a little word, but it contains so much emotion. It's something that I'm afraid we don't often feel anymore. But I'm sure you've felt it. At least I hope you have. I bet you can think back to a time when you felt safe. You felt warm, loved, and excited. You had an almost overwhelming enthusiasm about the very moment you were in, and you smiled. It almost felt like the sun was shining…but it was shining from you, rather than on you. Yeah. Remember that time when you smiled and you just couldn't help it? That's joy!

If you don't remember what joy feels like, or if even if you've never felt joy at all, it's not too late. Now is the time. It's time to go find it. Let yourself wonder. Make yourself wonder, without fear. Wonder is the first creation. It's the first step. Wonder is creating what you want in your mind—that life that brings you joy. Don't worry about the second creation—the physical creating. It will come on its own if you just let yourself fearlessly wonder.

So, set down your phones, or better yet…stack 'em all up. Set down the remote. I promise that your life won't be better because you know what's happening on a "reality" TV show. Set off on that adventure, that exploration. Choose your path. Exercise that God-given human freedom. Find your joy. Create your joy. And don't forget to enjoy the now; enjoy the journey you're embarking on.

Wonder.

Explore.

Discover.

Accept.

Smile.

46

You Aren't Angry

This isn't semantics, guys, so grab some chips and dip, and let's dig in.

Words are powerful. Words hurt people and heal people. Words start wars and end them. And although this post might initially seem like a play on words or a clever attempt to get you to see something from a new point of view, it really isn't. Take a moment to breathe while you read through this one. This subtle but important shift in the way we see (or say) things has helped me through countless episodes of depression, frustration, heartache, and disappointment.

Words, in and of themselves, can't actually hurt anyone. They are just sounds. These sounds are created by changes in air pressure made by the movement of our jaws, the shape of our lips and our tongues, the volume and rate of air passing through our throats and the frequency of the vibrations coming from our larynx.

But these changes in frequency and pressure can make you cry tears of heartache or tears of joy…so we do need to recognize and respect the power that they have.

Saying something, verbalizing…naming something…it somehow makes it more real. Hearing someone say, "I love you" matters. Hearing someone say, "I hate you" matters. But I'm going to ask you to be very mindful of something we all say far too often. Maybe as these days and weeks turn into months and years, we can create a healthier relationship with our words, our labels, and our emotions.

Pay attention to how often how often we say "I am…" then follow those two words with an emotion…an adjective…such as angry, happy, or frustrated. We are not adjectives. We are complex spiritual beings experiencing this human life.

So let's see what happens when do our best to stop saying, "I am angry," "I am sad," "I am aggravated," or, "I am happy!" Let's stop tying ourselves to ever-fleeting emotions, especially those that don't serve us.

If we "are angry," let's first recognize our emotion as such. Then, when describing how we are actually feeling, let's say, "I'm feeling pretty sad right now," or, "Oh my gosh! I feel so happy right now!" The difference between "being" and "feeling" is pretty significant.

Honestly! Stop for ten seconds right now. Think about how you are feeling. Are you feeling happy or sad? Excited or nervous? Grateful or resentful? Then once you have identified the emotion that you are most prominently experiencing, say this out loud: "Right now I am feeling…" then use the appropriate emotion.

"Right now I'm feeling very disappointed."

Then I want you to try to share how you are feeling with others as opposed to telling them how you are.

Maybe we can even start asking people how they are feeling rather than asking them how they are.

Saying, "I'm feeling disappointed right now" may seem like a small difference from, "I am disappointed." But recognizing the difference between who you are and what you are feeling, and giving power to the difference between them can bring you peace. It can make what feels like a painful situation fall in line as it should...a temporary emotion that certainly will pass.

We aren't sad or miserable or happy or elated. If we were, when our emotion changes...when the sadness goes away...that would mean we go away too. We certainly know that is not the case.

Like with every new habit, it will take a moment to learn that we are not our emotions. But we can coach each other through it.

I love you guys.

Five words.

Dad

47

Be Humble. Be the Salt.

"Do you wish to rise? Begin by descending. You plan a tower that will pierce the clouds? Lay first the foundation of humility."
— Saint Augustine

H ey guys! It's Dad.

This is a quick one, but boy has it stuck with me! It's about humility (being humble), and a simple strategy or point of view that will help keep us humble all the time.

Like everything else he's done, I've really enjoyed the book *Think Like a Monk* by Jay Shetty. The author wrote hundreds of pages, but a few things really stuck out to me. This is just one of them.

First of all, why is humility such an admirable character trait? In short, people aren't drawn to or attracted to vanity, pride, arrogance, or conceit. We love a humble champion. The basketball player who thanks her mom, her coaches, and her teammates for her success. "I'm so happy!

So grateful! I couldn't have ever made it here without the support of the rest of the amazing ladies on my team." Or the actor who wins an Academy Award and thanks the screenwriters for such an inspiring script.

There's something beautiful about sharing the spotlight...or even stepping out of the spotlight, smiling, while the others bask in the glory of their success. There's a real richness to that type of joy. That kind of joy...those types of memories last forever.

But when we win, when we thrive, don't we want to get excited and celebrate? You bet! Absolutely!!! But your humility will make those celebrations (and those around you) really sink deeply into your hearts.

Jay Shetty, taught by a monk, wrote, "Be like salt." When we think of salt, we typically think of it in terms of our food. If our food is too salty or if it's not salty enough...we notice. We think about it. We even complain about it. But if the salt level is absolutely perfect, if the chef nailed it...we don't even notice. When the salt level is right, we say that the food was good. Not the salt. The food. The meal was delicious. Even, "Wow! The seasoning is absolutely perfect."

Salt will never be in the spotlight. The salt makes everything it touches...better.

Be like salt, guys. Shine the light on others, then feel the energy of their joy flowing right into your hearts.

I love you guys!

#5Words

Dad

Acknowledgments

Learning fosters growth, and growth should be shared. When I started reading the touching comments left by friends, family, and followers on my Harvesting Insights and #itsdad blog and social media posts, I was dumbfounded. These authentic and vulnerable comments, text messages, and emails have been the encouragement I've needed to continue sharing my thoughts and ideas.

Thank you to those who've inspired and encouraged me. Here are a few comments that really left me thinking, *This journey? This...project? It matters. C'mon, Blasquez, don't let your insecurities derail something that's clearly reaching and speaking to others. This is what you're supposed to be doing.*

- "Sitting in public reading this, and yet again, you have reduced me to tears through your eloquence and strength to say what most of us ignore. Andy, you are an inspiration." ~ Andrew B.

- "Where do you get it? Where do you get the strength? Is it spite?...to keep giving of yourself? To keep pouring out the good despite the considerable challenges and heartaches that your life has thrown your way? I'm speechless. Speechless and inspired." ~ Taylor B.

- "Bless you for your transparency, your genuineness, and your never-ending desire to help others and make the world a better place." ~ Andrea L.

- "This is powerful stuff! As someone who struggles similarly to you, I'm very thankful for your openness and transparency. My tool kit looks very similar, and as I age, the dark and scary days are fewer and farther between. Thank you so much." ~ Kim C.

- "Thank you for your amazing words of wisdom! I want my kiddos to read this as I know they would benefit. What an inspiration you are with your words and how you live your life as a person, a teacher, and a father!" ~ Paula B.

- "I really enjoy your writing. It truly is inspiring and eye-opening. It gives us a moment to think and reflect! It's hitting a few nerves, so I call that success!! You're an excellent writer." ~ Doreen H.

- "Why can't the whole world have a heart like yours?" ~ Barbi F.

- "So thoughtful and well-written, Andy. I respect your articulations, and I love your heart." ~ Rebecca D.

About the Author

Andy Blasquez is a veteran middle school and high school teacher, adjunct professor, and single dad to his two sons. He is passionate about experiencing and exploring new things, learning, growing, then sharing what he's learned. He is also a writer, speaker, and animal rights and environmental wellness advocate.

With a bachelor's degree in Business Administration from California State University, Hayward, and a master's degree in Curriculum Design and Instruction from Chapman University, Andy possesses a unique blend of formal education and practical, real-world experiences. This unique blend of experiences leaves him ideally suited to convey clear, concise, inspiring, and memorable messages to his readers.

Andy demonstrates his ability to pull key concepts from an overwhelming volume of theoretical and practical information, then share that information in a way that ultimately reaches his audience. His writing style's engaging nature and conversational tone ensure that readers retain the intended messages long after the book goes back on the shelf or, better yet, gets passed on to the next reader.